2ND EDITION

I DARE TO DREAM PROJECT

idaretodreamproject.com   @idaretodreamproject

WHAT DO YOU DARE TO DREAM?

Submit a video sharing your dreams
and be a part of our documentary

    www.idaretodreamproject.com

@idaretodreamproject

#WHAT DO YOU DARE TO DREAM
www.idaretodreamproject.com

UNAPOLOGETIC PRESS
55 West 116th Street, PO Box 256
New York, NY 10026
Email: info@unapologeticpress.com

Dare to Dream Books are available at special discounts when purchased in quantity for premiums and promotions as well as fundraising or educational use. Special editions can also be created to specification.

For details, contact **info@unapologeticpress.com** or the address above.

INTERIOR LAYOUT & DESIGN: Unapologetic Press
AUTHOR'S PHOTO: Monica True

ISBN 978-1-945106-12-5 paperback
ISBN 978-1-945106-01-9 hardcover

Library of Congress Cataloging-in-Publication Data
is on file at the Library of Congress

to the "unrealistic, unpractical" visionary they call dreamer, let them talk while you relentlessly pursue your dreams

to Ed Dowling, for your friendship
and unwavering support

to Bob Howitt, for being curious about
the stranger sitting next to you and
for believing in the idea

THE DREAMER'S MANIFESTO

(*bold, sometimes rebellious, call to action)

DARE
— TO —
DREAM

2nd Edition

VALERIE JEANNIS

UNAPOLOGETIC PRESS

Contents

DARE TO PURSUE

WHAT IF I TRAVEL TO ALL 50 STATES INTERVIEWING SUCCESSFUL WOMEN IN ORDER TO EMPOWER YOUNG WOMEN?

That was the idea that kick started this journey and that eventually led to *I Dare to Dream Project*, a movement – with a powerful documentary at its core – daring women and girls to pursue their dreams unapologetically.

It was March 2010 and I was at a conference taking notes when the idea came to me. I was so excited, I immediately shared it with the stranger sitting next to me, because apparently, that's just what you do, *at least that's what I did.*

Her response? "That's a great idea, but you don't have any money."

How she came to that conclusion, I will never know. But she spoke my fears and I agreed with her. And just that quickly, I gave in to doubt.

I went on to do other things, including becoming an author, publisher, motivational speaker and trainer. However, I delayed going after *that* dream for over seven years – all because I chose to believe someone else's opinion.

Fortunately, the dream and the desire to empower women refused to die. Unfortunately, when people tell us we can't, too often we believe them and walk away from our dreams.

I'm on a mission to change that.

I believe in dreams. I believe they matter. I believe they're necessary and that they're fundamental in our search for purpose, direction and self-worth. I also believe in dreamers.

YOUR DREAM MATTERS

One dream, one simple idea can change the world or maybe a generation. But even if it only changes your life or the life of one other person, it's worth it. Your dream is your baby, your unique assignment and a gift entrusted to you, which is why it's up to you to stand for your dream and to find a way to make it a reality.

Dare to Dream started out as a reminder and message to myself that is now a message to *you*, the dreamer – **refuse to allow people, fears or circumstances to dictate what's possible for you and to keep you from pursuing your dreams.**

Is it amazing when people believe in you? *Absolutely*. Do you want the support of friends and loved ones? *Without a doubt*. However, if they doubt or tell you that you can't, I dare you to *do it anyway*. Dare to dream, then dare to pursue your dreams *unapologetically*. Because you can. Because you must. Because why not.

DARE TO DREAM

idaretodreamproject.com ⊙🅕🅕 @idaretodreamproject

DARE TO BELIEVE THAT YOU CAN BE, DO, HAVE, OR CREATE WHATEVER YOU CAN IMAGINE

DREAM WITH NO SHAME, NO REGRET, NO APOLOGY FOR WANTING WHAT YOU WANT OR FOR YOUR WILLINGNESS TO **GO FOR IT**.

DECIDE WHAT YOU WANT

What do you dare to dream?
Not what do you think you can get or what do
  other people, like your parents or friends want
  for you, but what's your dream?
I mean really, what do you want?

What do you dare to imagine that you can be,
  do, have or create?
What impact do you want to have in the lives of
  others?
What do you want your life to look like? to feel
  like?
What kinds of experiences do you want to have?

If you didn't care about other people's opinion,
If "they" never said it wasn't possible,
If "they" never said you couldn't,
If "they" never said you shouldn't,
And PS. Sometimes "they" is really you hiding
  behind the excuse of someone else...
What would you be doing?
What would you have attempted?
What would you attempt today?

What if you gave yourself permission to fail?
What would you love to try?

What would you love to try again?
To pursue again?
To ask for again?

What would you walk away from?
Who? When?
How would you show up differently?
More authentically?

What do YOU want?
What do you REALLY want?
What do you dare to dream?
An Invitation to Dream, Valerie Jeannis. 2017.

[PAUSE.]
Before you go to the next page, stop and actually think about the questions raised.

"What do you dare to dream?" is a fairly simple question, but one that many of us have a hard time answering. In our minds, that question somehow gets converted to, *"Based on what I have, where I am, what people think about me, and what I've seen those around me accomplish, what do I think I can get?"* And so, we settle while keeping our true dreams and desires hidden in our hearts.

That's why my challenge to you is to **dare to dream***, dare *to believe that you can be, do, have, or create whatever you can imagine.* Refuse to allow where you are to limit the magnitude of your dream, whether you decide you want to do something big or "small".

Just because you don't know how your dream will happen, does not mean that it can't happen.

IT'S POSSIBLE

I'll never forget the day I was told I'd get to take seven members of my family to Disney World. It was August 2009 and I was in Scottsdale, Arizona attending my first personal development conference. During one of the sessions, the presenter shared a story about how someone turned their bucket list into a large bulletin, placed it where others can see, and because of that received support to make one of his dreams happen.

As I was listening to that story, I remember looking around the room full of CEOs, executives and entrepreneurs and thinking, *"If I was ever going to share my bucket list, this would be the room to share it in.*" The fact that I didn't have a list did not stop me from asking the presenter if I could share that non-existent list with the other 300 attendees. To my surprise, I got a yes!

That night, I stayed up for hours asking myself "what do I want" over and over. I included as many specific things as I could think of on a folded 8.5 x 11 sheet of paper and made 300 copies.

True to their word, the staff distributed my makeshift bucket list pamphlet to everyone. Then the most amazing thing happened – an attendee tapped me on the shoulder and said, "I can do this for you."

One of the things on my list was to travel to Disney World with seven members of my family and stay at a five-star hotel.

He said, "I don't have a five-star hotel, but I can do this for you."

As I stared at him, he asked me, "What do you want?"

"I want to go to Disney World with seven members of my family."

"You already have that. What else do you want?"

"I want eight round trip plane tickets."

"Ok, what else do you want?"

"A Disney ticket for everyday we're there."

"Ok, what else do you want?"

At that point, I responded, "What?! There's more?!" To which he responded, "If you don't know what you want, then don't ask."

To which I immediately responded, "Wait, we need food!"

He then looked at me, nodded and asked, "When do you want to go?"

I was starting graduate school in two weeks and the main thought going through my mind was, *if I say next year, what are the chances I will get this trip?* So, I said next week *without even knowing what anyone else's plans were.*

One week later, my family and I were in Orlando, Florida, experiencing Disney World and staying at this beautiful 7-bedroom summer rental house in a gated community. In return, *all* this man wanted was that I never share with anyone who he was. That's it.

According to my circumstances I should have never been in Disney World, and yet, there I was.

That trip proved to me that "the impossible" can happen, especially when you **make time to decide what you want and then share it with others.**

SHARE YOURS

Our dreams and ideas live and die in the same place our fears grow and thrive – in our minds. However, when we speak our dreams out loud and share them with others, they're more likely to become a reality and when we speak our fears out loud, we're better able to confront them.

That's why **I'm producing a documentary inviting you to share your dreams.** You never know who will hear your dream and want to support you or how your dream will inspire someone else.

To be a part of the documentary project, record a video using your phone or camera answering three questions:

1 What do you dare to dream?

2 When it comes to your dreams, what are your fears?

3 What motivates you to pursue anyway?

Once you record your video, go to the website, **idaretodreamproject.com,** upload it and submit. That's it. **#whatdoyoudaretodream**

THE BREAKDOWN

To support you on your journey, *Dare to Dream* is broken down into three sections, each centered on one main question.

1 **DARE TO DREAM**
   Question: What do you dare to dream?

2 **BREAK UP WITH FEAR**
   Question: When it comes to your dreams, what are your fears?

3 **DARE TO PURSUE**
   Question: Will you dare to pursue your dream?

My goal is to challenge you with questions to think about and actions to take that will support you in defining and pursuing your dreams.

The pursuit is not always easy and it does come at a cost, but if you go for it, you will never have to wonder, "*What if I tried?*" Instead, you will talk about the years you dared to dream and pursue, and will share the stories of what happened after you said yes.

NOW WHAT

1. **FILL IN THE BLANK**. *write your own definition.*
   TO DARE TO DREAM IS _____

   _____

2. **FOOD FOR THOUGHT**
   - What are you hoping to get from the book?
   - What made you decide to read it?
   - What's really keeping you from going after your dreams?
   - What stopped you in the past?
   - What stops you today?

3. **WRITE YOUR OWN BUCKET LIST.**
   There are so many approaches to writing a bucket list. One is to come up with a list of 20 things you want to be, 20 things you want to do, 20 things you want to have, 20 things you want to create.

4. **WHAT DO YOU DARE TO DREAM? #shareyours.**
   Record and upload a video sharing what you dare to dream at **idaretodreamproject.com** and be a part of the documentary.

HOW TO
Dare to Dream

1   **DECIDE WHAT YOU WANT.** Not what others want for you. Not what you think you can get based on what you have and where you are. But what *you* really want.

2   **BE UNAPOLOGETIC.** Stand up for your dream. Make no apologies for your dream or your willingness to boldly pursue.

3   **DON'T BE A DELUSIONAL DREAMER.** Know what it takes and be prepared to do what it takes to make your dream a reality.

4   **BREAK UP WITH FEAR.** Make what you want more important than what you're afraid of and refuse to allow fear to keep you from pursuing.

5   **DON'T BE A FUNCTIONAL DEPENDENT.** Make your own choices and decisions, even if they're unpopular.

6   **BE AN EXTRAORDINARY FAILURE.** Embrace failure knowing that it's a part of the process. Learn, grow and keep moving forward.

7 **TAKE DRASTIC MEASURES.** Don't allow your challenges to stop you. Make them work for you by using out-of-the-box, unconventional strategies.

8 **K.I.S.S. YOUR DREAMS.** Simplify. Simplify. Simplify. Don't make things complicated when they don't have to be. *Keep It Super Simple.*

9 **GO FOR GREAT.** Give your best to the pursuit holding nothing back.

10 **BE UNQUENCHABLE.** Make up your mind that no matter what, you will birth your dream and make it a reality.

REFUSE TO ALLOW YOUR CIRCUMSTANCES TO DICTATE WHAT'S POSSIBLE FOR YOUR LIFE.

DREAMS DON'T CARE
GET DESPERATE

"Does a dream even matter?" That was the question she asked me.

In a time when people are satisfied to just make it through the day or when many aren't even pursuing their dreams, but seem to be doing ok, is it really necessary to 'dare to dream and dare to pursue our dreams'? *Does a dream even matter?*

Absolutely, unequivocally, without a doubt - *YES.* Dreams matter.

There was a time when my dream and my sincere prayer to God was for a Section 8 government subsidized apartment in a nice neighborhood because in my mind that was a step up from "the projects" where I was living. There was a time when I sat my mom and stepdad down with my then fiancé beside me and explained to them I didn't need to go to college because I already knew what I was going to do with my life – I was going to be a supportive wife and work with my husband as he traveled as a preacher. There was a time when I made up my mind I wouldn't go anywhere a car couldn't take me because I was afraid of dying in the air or drowning in the middle of the ocean.

For years, my life and aspirations were dictated by what I saw in my environment and what people saw for me, until the day I found the courage to call off my wedding and end that relationship, *a journey I share about in my first book, I Am Beautiful: Finding the Confidence to Pursue My Dreams.* At the time, I didn't realize how significant that decision was going to be. While it was the best decision, it was not an easy transition. I spent most of my days that year in bed and under the covers because I felt so lost.

All my plans were built around this one person and with him no longer there, I didn't know what was next for me. Worse, I didn't know who I was anymore or what I wanted.

One night, in the midst of my desperation, I prayed, *"God, there has to be more to life than this. There has to be more than the life I'm living."*

A few weeks later the answer to my prayers came when I was presented with an opportunity to study abroad in Paris, France.

Have you ever been so desperate you were willing to face your biggest fears in order to make a change?

As much as I was afraid of flying, the life I was living was no longer an option for me. I decided to face my fears and go. I placed my bachelor's degree on hold, resigned from my job, stepped down from every leadership position I occupied and kissed my mother goodbye. Within two months I was living in Paris.

It was that trip, on the other side of the world, in a place I've never been, among people I didn't know, who spoke a language I didn't fully speak, that taught me the secret to daring to dream – **your circumstances cannot dictate what's possible for your life**.

IT'S POSSIBLE

There are so many things we want that we convince ourselves isn't possible because of our circumstances, but *what if it has nothing to do with where you are or what you have?* ***What if you are just scared or too comfortable to make a change or go after what you really want?***

No one could have convinced me that Paris would've been a part of my story and there was nothing in my or my mother's bank account that suggested it would be possible for me to live abroad for a year. Yet, there I was.

During one of my two trips back home that year, I remember sitting in the window seat of the plane and looking at the lights from the houses below. As I watched the landscape, I prayed, *"God, even the biggest house is just a box from up here. Since it's all the same to You, I would like a big box too please."*

No longer was I praying for a section 8 apartment. What I really wanted was to own my own brownstone or townhouse. **Even though I didn't know how it would happen, I knew it was**

possible and that it was possible *for me*. That was enough for now.

What have you convinced yourself is not possible because of your circumstances? What are you settling for? What do you really want?

YOU NEVER KNOW

When I was asked, *"Does a dream even matter?"*, these were the thoughts that immediately came to mind.

Had it not been for a dream, I would have accepted marrying someone I did not want to marry and who did not have my best interest at heart. Had it not been for a dream, I would have accepted a life defined by others and my circumstances. Had it not been for a dream, there wouldn't have even been a plane for me to be afraid of!

It took desperation and an immense dissatisfaction with the life I was living to bring me to a place where for the first time, without the influence of anyone I knew or anyone who thought they knew me, I asked and answered two life-changing questions that I now challenge you to answer – **What do you want? And who do you want to be?**

When you dream, you have an opportunity to create the world, your world, the way you want it to be instead of simply accepting things as they are or letting whatever happens happen. That's why you have to learn to dream based on what's possible and not based on what you have.

You have to develop an attitude that in the face of doubt confidently responds, *"Why not and why not me?"*

Does a dream even matter? Absolutely yes.

Dreams are the places where we fly.

Dreams don't care who you are or what people think about you. Dreams don't care where you're starting from or how long you've been there. Dreams don't care how many times you may have failed or gotten it wrong in the past. Dreams have no limits and they go across all borders. They're ours if we want them. The question is, *will you dare to dream? And if so,* **#what do you dare to dream?**

NOW WHAT

1 FILL IN THE BLANK.

LIFE – DREAMS = _____

LIFE + DREAMS = _____

2 FOOD FOR THOUGHT.

- In your opinion, does a dream really matter?
- Is there anything you want that you convinced yourself is not possible because of circumstances?
- How can pursuing your dream change your life?

3 WHAT DO YOU DARE TO DREAM? #shareyours.

Record and upload a video sharing what you dare to dream at **idaretodreamproject.com** and be a part of the documentary.

HOW TO GIVE YOURSELF A
Reality Check

1 **ASK THE HARD QUESTIONS.** Are you really desperate for change? If so, how desperate are you?

2 **BE HONEST WITH YOURSELF.** What are you feeling? What are you unhappy about?

3 **TAKE RESPONSIBILITY.** What role do you play in creating the situations you're unhappy with?

4 **BE HONEST WITH OTHERS.** Is there anyone you're avoiding having a conversation with because it's scary or uncomfortable?

5 **PAY ATTENTION TO CLUES AND SIGNS.** What clues have life been giving you, whether it's from people, your body, environment, etc....?

6 **BE WILLING TO MAKE HARD DECISIONS.** What decisions have you been delaying? What next steps do you need to take?

7 **BE OPEN TO FEEDBACK.** Have you dismissed feedback you might need to reconsider?

8 **LOOK AT YOUR PATTERNS.** How do you avoid things that are difficult or uncomfortable?

9 **DO THE THING THAT SCARES YOU.** What have you been avoiding because of fear? What steps can you take to move forward?

10 **TRUST.** Do you know that regardless of what happens you're strong enough to handle it? Do you know that the support you need is available for you? (*PS. You are and it is.*)

REGARDLESS WHO DOUBTS OR CHALLENGES YOU, YOU HAVE TO BE PREPARED TO STAND FOR YOUR DREAM...

UNAPOLOGETIC NOT DELUSIONAL
STAND FOR YOUR DREAM

Unapologetic is an attitude
A necessity for every dreamer
It's the attitude of the ones who dare

It's about giving yourself permission to dream
the dreams of your heart and not a
watered-down version created based on
people, fears or circumstances
A watered-down version created to make
someone else happy or comfortable

Unapologetic is an attitude
A necessity for every dreamer
It's a no shame, no regret, no apology attitude
for wanting what you want and going after
what you want without compromising who
you are
It's a refusal to allow where you are to limit the
magnitude of your dream and your pursuit

Unapologetic is an attitude
A necessity for every dreamer
It's a frame of mind
A no-matter-what decision
A posture of determination and confidence

It's about giving yourself permission to be you
Permission to own your voice and own your
extraordinary
To own your gifts, talents, abilities, quirks, even
those pesky fears and insecurities as you're
working on eradicating them
It's about giving yourself grace as you figure it
out

Unapologetic is an attitude
A necessity for every dreamer
It's a decision to care less about other people's
opinions and judgments 'til you don't care
at all
It's breaking up with fear by making what you
want more important than what you're
afraid of

It's a decision to come out of hiding
To come out of the shadows and out from
behind someone else
It's a willingness to stand out, be seen and be
heard

It's showing up in a way others automatically
take notice of
Showing up in a way that says –
Are you looking? No? Well pay attention!

Unapologetic is NOT about being seen just to
be seen
Or speaking just to speak
Or being controversial to go viral

*It's about truly understanding that you can
     make a difference*
*That there are lives connected to your follow
     through*
*That someone needs to hear what you have to
     say, read what you have to write,
     experience what you have to share*

*It's about understanding that along the way it
     may get hard and you may be
     misunderstood or judged*
Yet in spite of all of that
Because of the purpose that drives you
You are willing to do it anyway
To pursue anyway
To say yes anyway
And to do it your way

Unapologetic is an attitude
A necessity for every dreamer
It's the attitude of the ones who dare

Catch it.
The Attitude, Valerie Jeannis 2018.

I'm going to tell you upfront that both you and
your dream will be challenged countless times
throughout this journey - by internal dialogue, *the
conversations in your head, negative self-talk, etc.*
and external pressures, influences and opinions.

There are those who'll be uncomfortable with
your boldness and audacity to dare to dream,
especially those who aren't living their dreams.

Some will have an attitude that says, *"Who are you to think that you can do this?"* *"Who are you to even want this?"* Others will give you their opinions about what your dream *should* look like or what a more *"acceptable"* dream for you would be.

Regardless who doubts or challenges you, you have to be prepared to stand for your dream because it is in fact *your* dream and *your* responsibility to bring to fruition. **If you don't, the consequences, regret and loss will be yours first, then it will be for every single person you were meant to touch and who needed what you had to offer.**

To stand for your dream you must be **unquenchable***. You must *refuse to be talked out of your dream by refusing to be satisfied, subdued or to settle for less.* And you have to make a **no-matter-what decision*,** to *decide from the beginning what the end will be and commit to that result.*

DON'T BE A DELUSIONAL DREAMER

If you were to look up the definition of the words dreamer and visionary, you would notice that it's not always seen as a positive thing to be a dreamer. According to *Merrian-Webster.com*, a dreamer is a person who is unpractical and idealistic, someone whose ideas or projects are considered audacious or highly speculative, a visionary. *Dictionary.com* defines visionary as one who tends to envision things in perfect but unrealistic form, an idealist, one who is given to impractical or speculative ideas, a dreamer.

Because others can't always see the vision, they may dismiss it and even classify you as a **delusional dreamer***, *someone with false or unrealistic beliefs and expectations about what it will take to make their dreams a reality*. That's why faith is so important and such an integral part of every aspect of this journey.

When no one else sees it and opinions tempt you to doubt yourself, it's your faith that reminds you it's possible and that encourages you to keep moving forward.

There's a thin line though between faith and delusion. Both are beliefs; however, faith is based on *good evidence and reason*, whereas a delusion is *a mistaken or misleading opinion or belief*. Understand the difference between the two and make sure that while you walk by faith, you are not a delusional dreamer.

NOW WHAT

1 FILL IN THE BLANK.

UNAPOLOGETIC IS _____

2 FOOD FOR THOUGHT.

- How has your dream ever been challenged?
- Did it change the way you felt about your dream?
- How do you apologize or hold back when it comes to your dreams?
- List three ways you can be more unapologetic.

3 CHEERLEADERS & CHALLENGERS.
You will always have people who cheer you on and others who will challenge you.

- Who are your biggest cheerleaders?
- Who tends to challenge your dreams?

4 WHAT DO YOU DARE TO DREAM? #shareyours.
Record and upload a video sharing what you dare to dream at **idaretodreamproject.com** and be a part of the documentary.

HOW TO NOT BE A
Delusional Dreamer

1   **DON'T KEEP YOUR DREAM IN YOUR HEAD.** Write it out. Talk it out. Share it with others.

2   **DON'T THINK THAT YOUR DREAM HAS TO BE BIG TO BE SPECIAL.** The worth of your dream is not determined by the size of your dream. So, dream true, whether it's big or "small".

3   **DON'T ASSUME.** Seek out good counsel and learn what it will take to make your dreams a reality based on where you currently are.

4   **HAVE MULTIPLE STREAMS OF INCOME.** Have a financial plan because financial stress can block creativity, delay progress, and most certainly kill dreams.

5   **DON'T BE CHEAP.** People will come along and help you, but this is *your* dream and *you* have to be willing to make the necessary investments of time, money, and resources.

6 DON'T THINK THAT FAITH AND SELF-CONFIDENCE ARE ENOUGH. "Faith without action is dead." James 2:17, *KJV*. Faith and self-confidence are important, but they are nothing without action. Start where you are and *do* what you can with what you have.

7 DON'T BE INCONSISTENT. Someone once said, "It's better to be consistently good than inconsistently great."

8 DON'T EXPECT TO BE AN OVERNIGHT SUCCESS. This journey is a process and chances are it will take longer than you think and require more than you expect. So, plan accordingly.

9 DON'T PUT YOUR LIFE AND RELATIONSHIPS ON HOLD UNTIL YOUR DREAM BECOMES A REALITY. Live your life as you pursue your dreams and make time for the people and things that are important to you.

10 DON'T PURSUE IF YOU REALIZE THE DREAM IS NO LONGER A FIT. It's ok to change your mind if what you're pursuing no longer lines up with what you want and who you want to be. Just make sure you're not changing your mind because of fear, doubt, or insecurity.

WHAT IF IT WASN'T ABOUT BEING RIGHT? WHAT IF YOU JUST GOT EXCITED BY QUESTIONS...? WHAT IF FINDING THE ANSWERS WAS AN ADVENTURE?

FOLLOW THE TRAILS

It starts with a dream
A goal, something bigger than you, that excites
and challenges you
It starts with a dream
One that pushes and stretches you to live outside
of your comfort zone
It starts with a dream
One that paints a new picture of what's possible
and what life can be like
It starts with a dream
A simple idea, which connects with the purpose
that lies inside of you and sparks and grows
into an unquenchable passion that leaves
you with no other choice, but to say yes
It Starts with a Dream, Valerie Jeannis, 2015

It all starts with a dream, but what do you do if you're not sure what your dream is?

For starters, relax. It's ok not to know. *But what if…? How? Who? What? When? Where? Why?*

So much pressure is put on having all the answers that we miss the most exciting aspect of questions – the discovery. Yes, a question is meant to elicit an answer, but it's also a seeking and the beginning of a discussion or journey.

What if it was not about being right? What if you started recognizing the potential that could be found in the quest that a question can lead you on? What if you just got excited by questions like, what do you want, who do you want to be, or what do you dare to dream? What if finding the answers was an adventure?

If you feel like you have a lot of options, then it becomes like a multiple-choice question or a game of elimination – *which one isn't it?* If you don't know what your options are, then it's more of a scavenger hunt where you're using what you do know to help you find and collect more clues. And as you collect the clues, like pieces in a puzzle, you'll start to see how everything fits together.

Regardless where you're starting, explore, pay attention to the clues and allow the process to take however long it takes.

To kick-start the journey, follow the trails.

FOLLOW YOUR PASSION

We all have things we're passionate about and that we naturally gravitate towards. As you pursue those passions, you'll start to see how one thing will often lead to something else you never really anticipated, which can eventually lead you to your dream and purpose.

Ever since I was eighteen years old, I've been passionate about empowering women and youth. At the time, I was in a difficult relationship I thought I'd never get out of. Because I didn't want to see other young women go through the same things or make the same mistakes I made, I started a mentorship group for those 13-15 year old. That group led to me pursuing both an undergraduate and master's degree in social work. Later, I decided that I wanted to start a residential non-for-profit organization (NPO) to help women aging out of foster care.

During graduate school, I reached out to one of my professors, Dr. Brown-Manning, who took the time to really listen. After I shared the vision of what I wanted the organization to look like, she asked me one simple question that put things in perspective for me – *Do you really want to start a NPO or are you trying to force your vision for something else into a NPO model?*

That conversation helped me realize I actually did *not* want to start a NPO, it was simply the only way I knew. **Often times we go down a particular path, not because we necessarily want to, but because we're not aware of the different options available to us.** That's why it's important to do research, to speak to others and to learn about other people's journey. As you do, you will start to see just how many possibilities are available to you.

After realizing I didn't want to start a NPO, I started searching and discovered I could start a business where I empower people as an author, speaker, coach and trainer, which is what I do today. All of this started with my passion to empower women and a decision to follow that passion even though I didn't know where it would lead.

What are you passionate about and what steps can you take today to start exploring those passions? Who can you reach out to for feedback and advice?

FOLLOW YOUR PAIN

If you ever looked into the origins of organizations such as To Write Love on Her Arms, Mothers Against Drunk Driving, and the Breast Cancer Walk, to name a few, you would discover they all started because of a pain the founder(s) or someone close to them experienced. While there are certain things we'll never fully understand when it comes to tragedy, **sometimes the hardest moments in our lives can reveal our life's call and purpose.**

There are defining moments after a tragedy when a decision must be made about what impact this event have in your life. *Will it be a catalyst for positive change? Or will you allow it to rob you of your joy and sense of purpose and keep you anchored to a moment in time?* As difficult as it can be and as deep as the pain often runs, **you can find purpose in pain.**

Think back to some of your most challenging moments. *What did those experiences teach you? Where you able to use what you've been through to help someone else? What kind of changes did* you notice needed to be made, either for you personally or in your community? Did you want to be a part of helping make those changes?

As you answer some of these questions, you will hopefully start to see that good can come from bad and that dreams can be conceived in the midst of pain.

FOLLOW ENCOURAGEMENT

Sometimes people will see greatness and potential in us before we see it in ourselves. The following is a snippet from an email I received from someone I met briefly at a conference years ago when I was still full of so many blanks and question marks.

Valerie,

I hope you find a way to inspire other women your age to never be afraid to stand tall and to be proud of who they are... Your gift is connection, showing others what can be done when you hold onto your desire with determination.

You dress the part of confidence; you also walk it and talk it. Share that passion with others who have fallen short of their dreams.

Maybe teach them through stories and examples, how self-creation and growth is possible, even from the lowest of low places.

If you could inspire one woman who was down and trapped in her life to stand up and take on life with all the courage and determination you have found throughout the country or even the world, what a wonderful gift that would be. Valor-ie

Looking back at some of the points made back then and what I'm doing today, it's obvious this person saw certain pieces of the puzzle before I did. When I get caught up in the fog of doubt and insecurity, I am reminded of words such as those, often spoken by strangers whose paths I crossed for a moment in time, but who saw things in me I didn't see in myself yet.

You cannot live on the words of people, but sometimes those words can serve as a lifeline until you're able to stand on your own faith and assurance of who you are and what's possible for your life. *What potential have people seen in you?*

If it's hard for you to see your gifts and talents or even if you think you already know what they are, interview people from different aspects of your life. Ask them what they see as your gifts, talents, and personal strengths.

Life is always giving us clues. Pay attention. Even if the clues aren't direct paths to your dream, remain open because they can bring you one step closer. You may find that the answers you're looking for are closer than you think.

NOW WHAT

1 **FILL IN THE BLANK.**

MY DREAM IS _____

2 **FOOD FOR THOUGHT.**
See the end of each section for reflection questions.

3 **LEARN THE STORIES OF OTHERS.**
Reach out to at least one person who inspires you and ask them about how they found their dreams/purpose. Be curious about their journey. There are some suggested questions included in the Companion Guide and Dare to Dream Workbook.

4 **SEE YOU THROUGH SOMEONE ELSE'S EYES.**
Get perspective from the different people in your life about the great things they see in you.

5 **SEE GOOD THINGS IN YOURSELF.**
Write out the things you love and admire about yourself. What are the different gifts and talents you see in yourself?

6 **WHAT DO YOU DARE TO DREAM? #shareyours.**
Record and upload a video sharing what you dare to dream at **idaretodreamproject.com** and be a part of the documentary.

HOW TO
Find Your Dream

1   **FOLLOW YOUR ACCOMPLISHMENTS.** What have you done that has given you the greatest sense of pride?

2   **FOLLOW YOUR COMPASSION.** Who do you want to help or make life better for?

3   **FOLLOW YOUR CONVERSATIONS.** What are you constantly talking about?

4   **FOLLOW YOUR CURIOSITY.** What are you curious about?

5   **FOLLOW YOUR DESIRES.** What do you want more of?

6   **FOLLOW YOUR ENTHUSIASM.** What excites and fuels you?

7   **FOLLOW YOUR FRUSTRATIONS.** What do you see or hear happening that really bothers you? What social problem would you change if you had the power?

8   **FOLLOW YOUR JOY.** What makes you happy? What seems to make time stand still for you?

9   **FOLLOW YOUR MONEY.** What do you spend your money on (*i.e., books, theatre, music, etc.*)?

10   **FOLLOW YOUR TIME.** What do you spend your time doing? What do you watch on TV? Beyond the drama, what is it about the show(s) that speaks to you or keeps you tuning in?

LIKE A SPARK THAT IGNITES A FOREST FIRE, AN IDEA, WHICH CONNECTS WITH THE PURPOSE INSIDE OF YOU, CAN GROW INTO AN UNQUENCHABLE DREAM THAT LEAVES YOU WITH NO OTHER CHOICE BUT TO SAY YES.

CONCEPTION OF A DREAM
BE OPEN TO POSSIBILITIES

Isn't it amazing how one moment can change your life? How something that seems so common or that you do all the time can start something so extraordinary without you even realizing it?

For Jaylene Clark Owens, her moment came in the form of a Facebook status update where she wrote, *"It's time to stop dipping a toe in here/ Wading in a little bit there/I need to jump back into this Sea World of poetry like I'm Shamu/ Heavy/ Too much gentrification going on in Harlem to get light/ Time to spit killer lines, with killer rhymes, of killer tales/ Cuz Harlem is looking more and more like the belly of a killer whale."*

Alfred Preisser, one of her former professors, saw the status update and asked her if she could create an entire show based on the killer whale/ gentrification metaphor that would incorporate theater and spoken word for his play reading series. Jaylene, who always wanted to create a show that blended her two loves, theater and poetry, jumped on the opportunity. What started out as a simple status update turned into an awarding-winning play with herself and three other friends that had sold out shows across the country.

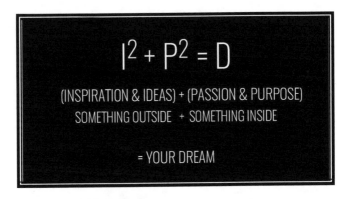

$$I^2 + P^2 = D$$

(INSPIRATION & IDEAS) + (PASSION & PURPOSE)
SOMETHING OUTSIDE + SOMETHING INSIDE

= YOUR DREAM

The **conception of a dream*** is *a process where something outside of you, an inspiration or idea, connects with something inside of you, your passion or purpose, and as a result of a continual yes, develops into a dream.* Like a spark that ignites a forest fire, **an idea, which connects with the purpose inside of you, can grow into an unquenchable dream that leaves you with no other choice but to say yes.**

In Jaylene's case, the request by her instructor to create a show based on her Facebook status (*something outside of her*) connected with her passions for theater and poetry (*something inside of her*) and the play, "In the Belly of a Killer Whale" (*the dream*), was conceived.

Without the influence of her professor, those words would have probably been just another good status update that eventually got filed away in the archives.

That's why it's important to interact with people and your environment and one of the main reasons why I love attending seminars and conferences. To be in a space with like-minded people from all around the world gathering with an open mind and open heart, people who are there to give as much as they are to receive, is beyond words. In fact, two of the major personal shifts in my life occurred while at seminars – the trip to Disney World and the inspiration for *I Dare to Dream Project*.

THE PLANTING OF A SEED

I never thought that taking the time to write a bucket list would have changed my life, but it did. After I received that trip to Disney World, I started looking at my list to see what else did I really want to go after. Some of the other things on my list included:

- Become an entrepreneur
- Empower women and youth
- Travel to all 50 states
- Interview entrepreneurs and CEOs

I didn't know how any of those things were going to happen and it didn't matter because I was reassured that the how would come. Sure enough, it did. Seven months later in March 2010, while taking notes at a seminar, I got the idea - *"What if I travel to all 50 states interviewing successful women in order to empower young women?"*

A concept from the seminar and the bucket list I wrote at the first conference (*something outside of me*) connected with my passion to empower women and youth and my desire to travel (*something inside of me*), and the idea for *I Dare to Dream Project* (*the dream*) was conceived.

A PASSING IDEA OR A DREAM WORTH PURSUING

All dreams start out as ideas, but not all ideas turn into dreams. Sometimes you'll just have this inner knowing. You'll have thoughts like, "*It just doesn't feel right*" or "*I just know that this is it*".

Just because you aren't always able to explain the feeling does not discredit its validity. It may not be enough for some people, but it should be for you, especially as you learn to trust yourself.

From the very beginning this is a walk of faith where you'll be making decisions based on what you believe, more so than on what you see or know for a fact. Sometimes it will be very obvious whether or not you should pursue a particular idea, other times not so much. Either way, you have to make a choice in order to move forward.

There are so many things that can impact the course of your life. Among those things is a dream, which starts out as an idea, that you dare to pursue.

NOW WHAT

1 FILL IN THE BLANK.
If you're considering an idea,
MY IDEA IS WORTH PURSUING BECAUSE _____

_____

2 FOOD FOR THOUGHT.
Has someone ever said any of the following or something similar in connection to your dream, gift or talent:

- Have you ever considered starting your own business ...?
- I would pay for that ...
- Others would pay for that...
- You should be a ...

3 WHAT DO YOU DARE TO DREAM? #shareyours.
Record and upload a video sharing what you dare to dream at **idaretodreamproject.com**.

HOW TO TELL IF AN IDEA IS
Worth Pursuing

1   **ENTHUSIASM.** On a scale of 1-10, how excited are you about this idea?

2   **PASSION.** Has the idea become a part of you? Is it constantly on your mind?

3   **PURPOSE.** Is it connected to your purpose?

4   **CREATIVITY.** Does it engage and capture your imagination? Can you work on it for hours without being mindful of time?

5   **COMMITMENT.** On a scale of 1-10, how committed are you to making your plans happen?

6   **PRIORITY.** Are you willing to change your plans to make it happen?

7   **CHALLENGES.** Are you willing to say yes in spite of challenges?

8   **INNER KNOWING.** Is there something inside of you saying, "yes this is it"?

9   **TIME.** Over time has your commitment to the idea gotten stronger?

10   **DESIRE.** Do you want to pursue this idea?

BREAK UP WITH FEAR

idaretodreamproject.com · @idaretodreamproject

CHOOSE TO MAKE YOUR
DREAM MORE IMPORTANT
THAN WHATEVER YOU'RE
AFRAID OF

D

CHOOSE TO NO LONGER ALLOW FEAR TO HINDER, CRIPPLE OR STOP YOU FROM PURSUING YOUR DREAMS.

CHANGE YOUR RELATIONSHIP WITH FEAR

Have you ever seen a child who's afraid to sleep because they believe they have monsters under their bed? Even though you know there really are no monsters, you can't deny their fears. Often, they're imagining things that aren't there or misinterpreting things that are.

As illogical as their fears can seem, they originated from somewhere and if they aren't properly dealt with, they can become a real hindrance.

When it comes to the fears that keep us from going after our dreams, they can be like monsters under the bed. We convince ourselves there's something out there to be afraid of and we allow those thoughts to influence and even dictate our choices.

Fear causes us to give up prematurely or to walk away without even trying. It suffocates our dreams, robs us of hope, and cripples our progress. Fear is also the main culprit behind the three major factors that cause us to consider aborting our dreams:

1 **THE PEOPLE FACTOR**, other people's opinions and judgments about you and your dream.

2 **THE CONFIDENCE FACTOR**, your own opinions and judgments about yourself, your dream and your ability to succeed.

3 **THE CIRCUMSTANCES**, external pressures and influences that makes pursuing challenging.

Which is the biggest fear factor for you? And are you allowing your fears to keep you from pursuing your dream?

BREAK UP WITH FEAR

We all have moments when we're afraid. However, when fear starts dictating your choices and holding you back, it's time to **break up with fear***, *to make a choice and a declaration to no longer allow fear to hinder, cripple or stop you from pursuing your dreams.*

Breaking up with fear is about changing your relationship with fear. It's about choosing to make your dream more important than what you are afraid of. It doesn't mean that fear will no longer show up or try to influence you. It does means that when it does, *and it will,* you can remind it and yourself of the choice you made to move forward in spite of.

EMBRACE FAILURE

One of the ways to break up with fear is to embrace failure. We convince ourselves we won't be able to handle failure. We say we cannot do something, not because we really doubt our ability to do it, but because we are afraid to try and fail. Or perhaps, we may have tried and failed in the past and we allow that to hold us back and keep us from trying again.

To dare to dream is to risk failure. There is no way around that. There will be times you go after something and you will miss the mark. In those moments you can choose to give up and think self-defeating thoughts such as, "*I knew I couldn't do this. Things never work out for me. They were right,*" or you can choose to be an **extraordinary failure***, *someone who initially falls short of an intended goal, but eventually gets what they want or something greater than they imagined because they did not give up the pursuit.*

To be an extraordinary failure is an honor few people receive because not everyone is willing to put themselves out there, fail, and still go after the same thing, even if they have to go after it a different way. **That's the extraordinary part, to be willing to try and try again with the sting of failure still fresh in your mind and the voice of doubt loud in your ears.**

The secret to embracing failure is to aim for the win, but to not make it about the win. Make it about the pursuit and recognize that as much as it's about the goal, it's also about the journey and who you're becoming along the way.

As painful and as frustrating as it was, I'm grateful for the things that didn't work out how I originally planned because so many great things, including this book, would have never happened. I'm *not* telling you to actually set yourself up to fail. What I *am* saying is you don't have to be afraid of failing because if and when you do, it can position you for something greater than you originally planned.

NOW WHAT

1 FILL IN THE BLANK.
FEAR IS _____

2 FOOD FOR THOUGHT.
When you think about pursuing us dream, which of the following are the biggest challenges for you?

☐ Wrong Time or Not Enough Time

☐ Lack of Funds

☐ No Support/lack of support

☐ Someone said it wasn't possible or that you shouldn't

☐ Being forced or pressured to do something else

☐ Afraid it will change things

☐ Don't think you can't do it

☐ Afraid you will fail

☐ Don't think that your idea is good enough

☐ Other: _____

3 WRITE A BREAKUP LETTER TO FEAR.
Follow the steps of how to break up with fear. Then, write a breakup letter to fear and submit it at **idaretodreamproject.com/dearfear**

HOW TO
Break Up with Fear

1. **CALL FEAR OUT.** Write out all of the fears that come up for you when you think about your dream. Be as specific as possible.

2. **CHECK THE SOURCE.** Where did your fears come from? An experience? Someone else? Something you heard or saw?

3. **CHALLENGE THE FEARS WITH TRUTH.** Have you or others overcome these specific fears or similar ones in the past? It helps to remember that fear can be conquered.

4. **PUT YOUR FEARS TO THE TEST.** Do the thing you're afraid of.

5. **HAVE A PLAN AND GET SUPPORT.** Some fears require a strategy. Reach out for support and create a plan to overcome your fears. You don't have to do it alone.

6. **COUNT THE COST.** What has fear or can fear cost you?

7   **FOCUS ON THE PRIZE.** What are you fighting for and what you stand to gain if you stand up to fear?

8   **BE PATIENT WITH YOURSELF.** There may be times you'll give in to the fear. Learn from those moments and then keep moving forward.

9   **CELEBRATE THE WINS.** Every time you take a step forward in spite of your fears, write it down and celebrate yourself, even if it's just taking a moment to literally give pat yourself on the back.

10 **WRITE A BREAKUP LETTER TO FEAR.** Write about how fear has influenced, changed, or hindered you. Then write about what will now be possible because you're choosing to make your dream more important than your fears. Submit your breakup letter online at **idaretodreamproject.com/dearfear** to be a part of the campaign.

YOU CANNOT ALLOW SOMEONE ELSE'S OPINION TO DETERMINE WHAT YOU CAN OR CANNOT DO OR WHAT YOU WILL OR WILL NOT DO. AT SOME POINT, YOU HAVE TO LEARN TO TRUST YOURSELF...

CARE LESS

I used to babysit my 2-year-old godson, who was incredibly hyperactive. One moment he would be sitting next to me, the next he would literally be half way up a cabinet. Because of that, I was always afraid he would hurt himself. Every time I didn't see him for a few seconds or he started getting up, I'd scream out his name in a panic and was constantly telling him no. I loved him and wanted him to be happy, but my priority was keeping him safe. It would have been easy for him to think I was being mean, but really, I was scared and trying to shield him from danger the best way I knew.

It's one thing when those in your life set out to hurt you. It's another thing when they hurt you while attempting to protect you. Depending on their personal experiences and perspective, there will be people you love and who love you, who'll tell you no or try to discourage you when it comes to your dreams. Though their hearts may be in the right place, parents tend to be guilty of this. In a misguided attempt to keep you safe, they may use their influence or relationship to force their dreams for you on you, often leaving you feeling powerless to go after what *you* really want. They may even go so far as to threaten to withdraw their financial support, especially if they know you're dependent on that support.

TRUST YOURSELF

Whether or not it is coming from a place of love, you cannot allow other people's opinion to determine what you can or cannot do (*your beliefs*) or what you will or will not do (*your actions*). At some point, **you have to learn to trust yourself and follow your heart**, which may be the hardest thing you learn to do.

I once ran into a beautiful actress in the fruit section of the supermarket. What started out as a simple hello turned into a conversation about life and choices. She shared how on the day of her wedding, she stood outside the church doors holding her father's arm. When the music started playing and her father was ready to take a step forward, she held him back shaking her head no.

Her dad looked at her and told her, "*Listen, I paid a lot of money and there are a lot of people sitting in there waiting for you. Come on.*" Even though she changed her mind and no longer wanted to marry this man and everything inside of her was screaming for her to run, she walked down the aisle anyway and said, "*I do.*"

When I asked her why, she responded, "*If my dad would've said, 'Baby, don't worry about it. If you don't want to do this, you don't have to. You go and I'll take care of everything else,' I would never have done it. But he didn't and I didn't know how to say no.*" Unfortunately, her doubts proved to be right. It took years for her to finally find the strength to do what she wanted to do on her wedding day – walk away.

On my way home that night, I couldn't help but wonder, *how many times do we do things in spite of ourselves? How many times do we feel uneasiness about people and directions we're getting ready to take, but we ignore it? How many times do we feel led down a certain path or change our minds about continuing down the path we are currently on, but we choose to ignore our inner voice and to listen to people instead? How many times do we have an idea or a dream that we want to pursue, but we allow someone else to talk us of it? Or to talk us into going after what they want us to pursue? How many times have you done it?*

VOICES IN OUR HEADS

Part of what keeps us from pursuing our dreams are the voices in our heads. Some of those voices include:

1   **THE VOICE OF AUTHORITY.** Often times we can value the opinion of those we respect above our own because of their positions or accomplishments. If they tell us we can't, too often we believe them. Or, we tend to follow their advice, even when we don't fully agree or when something inside of us is saying to pursue a different route.

2   **THE VOICE OF LOVED ONES.** Though they may have good intentions, the feedback of friends and loved ones can at times lead to doubt and stress. They can discourage you from pursuing your dream, try to encourage you down a path *they* feel is best for you, or try to limit you or make you feel guilty for wanting what you want.

3   **THE VOICE OF DOUBT.** The voice of doubt is the voice of fear. It usually speaks from negative past experiences or our own limited view or opinion of ourselves and our abilities. It will always try to talk you out of taking leaps of faith and into playing it safe, even when it's painful.

In the midst of the voices of negativity, you also have your inner voice, the part of you that seems to know the answers to the questions even if you can't always logically explain why that's the answer. Your inner voice leads, guides, teaches, prompts, inspires and urges you by showing you what to do, when to do it and who to partner with. Some think it's the universe speaking to them; I believe it's the Creator of the universe. Unlike the other voices, your inner voice speaks from a place of faith and possibility and reminds you of who you are and what you can do.

We are divinely guided people and are continuously given insight regarding situations and questions we have. We just have to become better listeners and more intentional about tuning in to our inner voice and internal guidance system.

One way to start recognizing your inner voice is by looking for patterns. Think back to different situations in the past when you had questions about a choice you had to make and you just knew what the right answer for you was. Even if you couldn't explain how you knew that was the right choice, you just knew. Regardless whether or not you listened, that was your inner voice. Think of other moments in your life when you had this similar sense of knowing. As you start to notice the patterns, it will become easier to distinguish your inner voice and to get answers to your questions. What you choose to do with that information is your choice.

THE POWER OF CHOICE

There was a time when you had to live according to the choices of others. You had to do what you were told, go where you were told, sleep when you were told, and eat what you were told. You are no longer a child and you can now exercise the **power of choice***, *the power to decide for yourself what you want in any given situation*.

But let's be honest, sometimes you want someone else to make the hard decisions for you. You want them to tell you whether or not you should go after your dream or down a certain path. That way, if things don't work out, you can just pass the blame.

Having someone else make the hard choices can feel easier. However, even when you try to blame someone else for *your* choice when you don't like the outcome, *you're* the one who has to live with the consequences. The "just tell me what to do" attitude and mindset will only make you a **functional dependent***, *someone who continuously allows others to make choices for them or who allows the choices of others to dictate their choices.*

Unless you want to delay your process or risk not pursuing your dream at all, you have to make decisions for yourself, even when it is unpopular or causes others to misunderstand you.

CARE LESS

There is a story told about a young boy who entered a barbershop where the barber whispered to his customer, "This is the dumbest kid in the world. Watch. I'll prove it to you." The barber placed a dollar bill in one hand and two quarters in the other, then called the boy over and asked, "Which do you want, son?" The boy took the quarters and left.

The barber turned to his customer and said, "What did I tell you? That kid never learns!"

Later, when the customer left, he saw the same young boy coming out of the ice cream store and asked him, "Why did you take the quarters instead of the dollar bill?" The boy licked his cone and replied, "Because the day I take the dollar, the game is over!"

It turns out the dumbest kid in the world might not be so dumb after all. Somewhere along the way he learned a lesson we all need to learn – *who cares what people think about you?* He was willing to look stupid and to accept people talking negatively about him in order to get what he wanted. *Are you willing to do the same?*

One of the reasons we have a hard time pursuing what we want when we know others want something else for us is because, whether or not we admit it, there are certain people whose approval we want and we don't want to feel like we are disappointing them. While that is understandable, you have to free yourself from the need for the validation of others.

If you want to freely pursue your dreams and to execute the different ideas that will help you actually birth those dreams, you have to make up your mind to care less.

Even when you actually do care, **people's opinions and validation cannot be more important to you than it is for you to actually be true to yourself and your dreams.** Besides, it takes too much energy to constantly be concerned about how people will respond. So, care less. It may be a mildly aggressive statement, but it's also a very liberating one.

Seriously, *does everyone have to agree with you? Does everyone have to think your idea is great? Does everyone have to be excited about what you're pursuing? Isn't it enough that you're excited? And if it isn't, shouldn't it be?*

FIGHT FOR IT

The pursuit of your dreams is not a democracy dependent on majority approval. People have the right to their opinions, just like you have the right to politely disagree and to move forward anyway. Even when it's unpopular, **find a way to stand for your dreams.**

And F.Y.I., fighting for you dream is *not* about fighting people, so don't waste your time trying to convince anyone of the validity of your dream. Instead, invest your energy in nurturing, protecting, and developing the dream that you are carrying.

And here is a little secret: When you stick to your decision and work to make your dreams a reality, many of your naysayers will be the very same ones who show up and tell you how great you are and how they knew you were going to make it the whole time. They will even offer their support. As tempting as it may be to roll your eyes or to remind them what they really thought, don't get bitter. Their doubt and negativity may have been the very motivation you needed to make the choices that were crucial to your success.

NOW WHAT

1 **FILL IN THE BLANK.**
THE LOUDEST VOICES IN MY HEAD ARE _____

_____

2 **FOOD FOR THOUGHT.**
- Whose opinion means the most to you?

- What do they think about your dream and your pursuit?

- Would you be willing to move forward regardless whether or not you have their blessing?

3 **WRITE A BREAKUP LETTER TO FEAR.**
Write a breakup letter to fear and submit it at **idaretodreamproject.com/dearfear**

HOW TO NOT BE A
Functional Dependent

1 **KNOW YOUR DECISION-MAKING PATTERNS.** Are they creating the results you want? If not, what do you need to do differently?

2 **STOP SEEKING APPROVAL.** You can't live for people or their approval.

3 **CARE LESS.** You're going to have to be ok with disappointing some people.

4 **DECIDE FOR YOURSELF.** Don't allow others to make your decisions for you. Be honest with yourself about what you want and then make a choice.

5 **RECOGNIZE THE IMPACT OF YOUR CHOICE.** The choices you make will impact others.

6 **MAKE THE HARD CHOICES.** Don't simply go with the flow because it's easier. Make the best choice even when it's uncomfortable or unpopular.

7 **BACK YOURSELF UP.** When others encourage you to do something you're not comfortable with, trust yourself.

8   **FOCUS ON THE BIG PICTURE.** Focus on your vision and the end goal and let that motivate you and dictate your choices.

9   **TAKE RESPONSIBILITIY**. Don't pass the blame if things don't go as planned.

10 **DON'T BE HARD ON YOURSELF.** Understand that you won't always get it right; however, things can still turn out better than you expect or planned.

PEOPLE WILL ALWAYS
HAVE AN OPINION ABOUT
WHO THEY THINK YOU
ARE AND WHAT THEY
THINK YOU CAN DO.
THEIR OPINIONS SHOULD
NEVER MATTER MORE
THAN YOUR OPINION OF
YOURSELF...

THE CONFIDENCE FACTOR
CHANGE THE WAY YOU SEE YOURSELF

On February 26, 2013, the day before my 28th birthday, I sat in a meeting and listened as someone I respected, questioned everything I was working towards, including my motives. Thinking back, I don't even remember exactly what was said. I just recall being taken aback to the point of tears.

After regaining my composure, I kept it together long enough to say thank you and then leave. While I'm sure it wasn't their intention, I felt like I was hit... **hard**.

I was devastated.

It wasn't the no itself, but who the no came from. They were my mentors. I trusted and looked up to them and they didn't think I could do it.

The crazy thing is, they never even said no.

They stole my faith with a no they never said
They stole my faith with permission
And I was vulnerable
Leaving my dream unguarded
Because faith was the shield from opposition
It was a shield from me

They stole my faith with a no they never said
They stole my faith with permission
And I was the one who gave them the key

How does that even happen?
They robbed me
But never touched me
Their doubt became my doubt
And my faith was dislocated

Without faith my dream was exposed
And the attacks came relentlessly –
People, fears and insecurities
It all threatened to overwhelm me
And as I scrambled to get out of reach of their
   arrows
I took my dreams and I went under
The No that Stole My Faith, Valerie Jeannis, 2017.

It was after that meeting I first went into hiding.

I became embarrassed by my dream. I was embarrassed for dreaming so big and for thinking I could ever be who I aspired to be and do what I aspired to do. That's when I started wondering if I was good enough. If anyone would want to help me, to join and be a part of the vision.

I became a perfectionist stuck in over-planning. Days turned into weeks and weeks into years. And I stayed hidden, but this time behind the cloak of success. I was traveling, speaking, writing, doing book signings. I even started my own publishing company, *Unapologetic Press*. In the eyes of others, I was a "success", but I knew I was holding back. Playing it safe and small and keeping one of my bigger dreams hidden. I was getting by with an external smile while filled with internal frustration.

I hid publicly, sidelined by fear, angry, down and hating the life I was living. All because I lost my faith. All because I gave it away.

They stole my faith with a no they never said
They stole my faith with permission
And I was the one who gave them the key
I made their opinions more important than my
    own
I made their opinions more important than God's
The No that Stole My Faith, Valerie Jeannis, 2017.

DISTORTED VIEW

People will always have an opinion about who they think you are and what they think you can do. None of those opinions will ever matter more than your opinion of yourself, which impacts *EVERYTHING,* from what you attempt to the way you interact with others to what you charge and earn. Because it's so important, if you struggle with self-doubt or insecurity, identify the sources and contributors.

1   **CHECK YOURSELF.** Do you tend to say negative things about yourself? Do you talk down your accomplishment? Do you dismiss or discredit compliments?

2 **CHECK WHAT YOU'RE LISTENING TO**. What kinds of music and lyrics are you constantly listening to or playing in the background? What kind of words and advice do you entertain?

3 **CHECK YOUR ENTOURAGE**. Who are you surrounding yourself with or constantly around? Are they positive or negative? Uplifting or depressing? Encouraging or demoralizing?

4 **CHECK YOUR ACTIONS**. Do your actions and the choices you make line up with what you say you want or do they contradict? Do you keep your word to yourself and to others?

5 **CHECK YOUR MINDSET**. Do you constantly compare yourself and your results to other people's? Do you disqualify yourself because of how well someone else has done? Do you believe you're worth it?

As you identify the negative influences, you can make changes that will immediately help you build your confidence. You can change the way you talk to yourself and about yourself, change the music and words you listen to, be more selective about who you hang out with and for how long, keep your word to yourself and stop comparing yourself to others.

You don't fully know who you are yet. If you look at a caterpillar, nothing about it suggests that inside of this creature there are wings. So ordinary looking, yet destined to fly. Whether you believe it yet or not, there's more to you than what meets the eyes and you'll discover that "more" as you pursue.

The pursuit of your dreams is a journey of self-discovery where you'll continuously discover who you are and what you are capable of.

You'll set out to accomplish one thing, and along the way you'll do so much more than you ever anticipated. You will conquer giants, challenge old, invalid beliefs, and discover new worlds both within and around you. You'll meet new people and form your own beliefs about what's true for you. Essentially, you'll discover and be reintroduced to yourself.

BEYOND A SHADOW OF A DOUBT

After the meeting on February 26th, all I wanted to do was get under the covers and sleep in the next day. Fortunately, that wasn't an option because I had a speaking engagement at an alternative high school in downtown Brooklyn.

Needless to say, I wasn't in the best frame of mind nor was I feeling particularly confident. It didn't help that I overslept and woke up with puffy eyes, that it was raining, and that I arrived to the school late. As rough as the day started, it turned out to be a day I'll never forget.

Have you ever had one of those moments when you knew beyond a shadow of a doubt that you were doing exactly what you were meant to do?

As I stood in front of those students, who were literally staring me down, I decided to just be myself. And while I was speaking, I watched as the students actually leaned in to listen to what I was saying. In that moment there was this knowing and absolute conviction that this is *exactly* what I'm supposed to be doing with my life.

It didn't matter others didn't see it yet or that I didn't know how it was going to work out. I just knew I was exactly where I was supposed to be.

I said it already and I'm going to say it again, people will always have an opinion about who they think you are and what they think you can do. None of those opinions will ever matter more than your opinion of yourself.

May you be your greatest ally.

NOW WHAT

1 FILL IN THE BLANK.

I AM _____

2 FOOD FOR THOUGHT.

- How has your opinion of yourself impacted your pursuit and level of success?

- Has someone else's opinion ever robbed you of your faith in yourself?

- Who inspires you to believe in yourself?

3 WRITE A BREAKUP LETTER TO FEAR.

Write a breakup letter to fear and submit it at **idaretodreamproject.com/dearfear**

HOW TO
Build Your Confidence

1 **REDEFINE YOURSELF.** Define who you want to be and what steps you can take to become that person.

2 **GIVE YOURSELF GRACE.** If you messed up or it takes you some time to figure certain things out, be patient with yourself.

3 **UPDATE YOUR OPINION OF YOURSELF.** Just because something was true before does not mean it's true today. *What old, outdated beliefs about yourself are you holding on to that you need to update?*

4 **ACKNOWLEDGE YOUR WINS.** Create an encouragement wall or a space where you make note of your accomplishments and thank yous received from others. Make it visual and public so you can constantly see it and be reminded of your progress and contributions.

5 **SEE THE BEST IN YOURSELF.** Make a list of 10 things you love and appreciate about yourself.

6   **SEE YOURSELF THROUGH SOMEONE ELSE'S EYES.**
See yourself through the eyes of someone who sees the best in you. Ask that person for feedback about the good things they see in you.

7   **CELEBRATE AND ACKNOWLEDGE YOURESELF.**
Daily take the time to answer the following "I'm proud of myself because..."

8   **REMIND YOURSELF WHY YOU CAN.** Create a list of at least 10 reasons why you know you can make your dreams a reality.

9   **BE SOMEONE ELSE'S CHEERLEADER.** Celebrate and acknowledge the great things you see in someone else. It helps to take the focus off yourself and what you're working on.

10   **REMIND YOURSELF WHY YOU MUST.** Sometimes we just need to remember that our dreams are bigger than us. Create a list of at least 10 reasons why you must make your dreams a reality.

CHALLENGES CANNOT STOP YOU. IT'S HOW YOU VIEW THOSE CHALLENGES THAT CAN GET IN YOUR WAY.

DON'T DISMISS YOUR IDEAS

Three days before she died of cancer, Sarah called her friend Jodie and begged Jodie to promise that she would pursue her dream of traveling around the world. Jodie felt torn because even though she wanted to promise her friend, she didn't want to lie. She tried explaining she didn't have the money to travel, but Sarah refused to take no for an answer.

"Promise," she said.

Jodie promised.

A few months later, Jodie, who originally said no to her dreams because of her lack of finances, left home and backpacked around the world for a whole year.

As I sat next to her and listened to her share her story, she turned to me and asked, *"Why does it have to take something like that to make us go after our dreams?"* At first, I didn't know what to say. In the end though, **it really comes down to one thing, a decision.** A conscious and intentional no-matter-what decision that refuses to allow people, fears or circumstances to keep us from pursuing our dreams. A decision to trust that someway, somehow, everything needed will manifest and be provided and that everything will work out.

We're really good at coming up with excuses about why we can't pursue. At the top of our list is usually lack of time, lack of money, and lack of resources. However, it's rarely a resource issue. It's often a mindset and decision issue.

If you're currently in a tight place financially, you may beg to differ, but challenges cannot stop you; it's how you view and handle those challenges that get in your way.

PROVISION WILL COME

Pursuing your dreams is a walk of faith where **provision follows the decision**. If you're waiting for money, people, time, or whatever else you convince yourself you need in order to start, then you may be waiting for something that will not come until after you start. You have to be so invested in making your dreams a reality that even with the odds against you, you're still willing to say yes and to take action. Provision will follow that kind of passion and commitment, and so will the people you need.

We frequently miss provisions when they come, because they don't show up the way we expect. Sometimes they show up as ideas. Since we get ideas all the time, more often than not, we dismiss them. We see them like pennies on the street, common and too small to be worth the effort. We forget that, like pennies, ideas are the foundation everything we see around us were built upon.

I DON'T KNOW AND NEITHER DO YOU

What can I say that will challenge you to give your ideas a chance? What can I say that will challenge you to not allow what you don't have to cause you to give up on what you want or on your ideas? I don't know. And in fact, that's the answer – I don't know and neither do you.

You don't know what will happen if you pursue. You don't know the difference it could make or the impact it could have. You don't know where it will lead you or who it will lead you to. You don't know if it's the missing piece to the puzzle you're trying to figure out. You don't know and you will never know as long as you keep dismissing your ideas as insignificant or making excuses for why your dreams can't happen.

DRASTIC MEASURES

Instead of allowing challenges to stop you, make them work for you by taking **drastic measures***, out-of-the-box, *unconventional strategies used to overcome challenges and create desired results.*

One underutilized strategy is **the art of asking***, a *willingness to ask the right people, seek in the right places and knock on the right doors for what you want adjusting your strategies as needed and remaining persistent until you get it.* It requires you to push past your insecurities, doubts and fears to ask for the help you need from the people you want and need it from.

Inspiration is another integral strategy. It helps you tap into creativity and possibilities you may not have considered. It also prompts you to ask and answer idea-generating questions like,

- *What if I …?*
- *Wouldn't it be great if…?*
- *Maybe I can …?*
- *How can I do something similar?*

To stay inspired, keep an **inspiration file***, *a collection of ideas, strategies and stories of how others are pursuing their dreams.* Expose yourself to new things and people and if you come across something that grabs your attentions, file it. Whenever you're working on something new or feel stuck, just pull out your file.

Drastic measures don't have to be these big elaborate strategies. Sometimes it's simple things that make huge differences. It really is about asking yourself what it will take to make your dreams happen given the challenges you have to deal with. It's about completion and involves an element of desperation that leaves no room for excuses and pushes you to the point where you're no longer concerned about the things that stopped you in the past.

Provision follows a decision and often comes in the form of ideas. So, list your ideas. Explore them. Decide if you want to pursue them. But do not simply dismiss them.

NOW WHAT

1 FILL IN THE BLANK.

INSPIRATION IS _____

2 FOOD FOR THOUGHT.

- What challenges and limitations are you currently facing when it comes to your dreams?

- Come up with at least 10 ideas for how you can overcome each challenge. Have fun with it.

3 JOURNAL OF IDEAS.

Carry a pocket size journal with you to jot down your ideas. Don't judge your ideas or filter them. Just write down whatever comes to mind whenever it comes.

4 WRITE A BREAKUP LETTER TO FEAR. share yours.

Write a breakup letter to fear and submit it at **idaretodreamproject.com/DearFear**.

HOW TO

Ask

1   **MAKE YOUR ASK CLEAR**. Be specific about what you want, who you would like it from and when you would like it. Don't reduce your ask to what you think you can get.

2   **BE FLEXIBLE**. Know when to take advantage of a great alternative offer.

3   **HAVE THE RIGHT ATTITUDE**. No one owes you anything. Be bold, but also be humble in your approach. How you ask, can and will influence your outcome. The wrong attitude can ruin incredible opportunities just like the right one can create them.

4   **DON'T ASSUME.** Reach out to people. You don't know how they'll respond. Even if the answer is no, it gives you a chance to follow up and ask for feedback and referrals.

5   **COLLECT NOS**. Instead of focusing on how many yeses you can get, set goals for how many nos you want to collect a day. It may seem a bit backwards, but it works.

6 **KEEP IT SIMPLE**. Make it easy for people to say yes with a simple request. Be clear, direct and strategic about what you ask for.

7 **FOLLOW UP.** When they say yes, know what the next steps you want them to take are.

8 **FOLLOW THROUGH**. Do what you said you'd do by when you said you would do it. If something comes up or you need to make a change, communicate.

9 **OFFER YOUR ASSISTANCE**. Don't assume you have nothing to offer.

10 **BE GRATEFUL**. Don't underestimate the power of gratitude. Make it a priority to appreciate those who support you along the way.

WHILE IT WOULD BE EASY TO BEAT YOURSELF UP WITH THE NEGATIVE QUESTIONS ... THOSE WILL NOT SERVE YOU AS MUCH AS THE "WHAT AM I GOING TO DO NOW?" QUESTION OR THE "WHAT DO I WANT TO DO NOW?" QUESTION.

IT'S NOT TOO LATE
DARE TO DREAM AGAIN

"I'm *** Miserable."

Personally, I don't curse; however, when that statement was made after I asked someone if they were happy, I almost felt like getting up and applauding.

It was so honest it was refreshing. The words jumped off the screen unapologetically and all I could type back in response was "*GREAT! Now what are you going to do about it?*"

When it comes to past dreams, if we're really honest with ourselves, we might be surprised by what shows up.

When you choose to walk away from your dream, not just a passing idea, but a dream that really connects with something inside of you, you do so at a risk. The most common aftermath you might experience are:

1   **THE WHAT-IF SYNDROME**, *when you are constantly taunted by the dream you gave up on and you fantasize about what could've been.* In one word, regret.

2   **RECKLESS BEHAVIOR**, *activities you engage in to either help you feel or help you forget.* It can range from foolish investments, destructive behavior, poor choices in

relationships and friendships to becoming a workaholic or even doing good because you feel so guilty.

3   **A CYCLE OF QUITTING**, repeat behavior. Once you walk away or give up on something that means so much, it can become easier to walk away from other important things or to keep giving up. Even when you want to do better, you can get in a cycle of quitting that will impact your confidence.

All of these can lead to a place of hopelessness where it starts to feel like nothing really matters. But it's not too late. You get to dream again.

NOW WHAT

While it would be easy to beat yourself up with the negative *"What if?"* questions or the *"Why did I?"* questions, those won't serve you as much as the *"What am I going to do now?"* question or the *"What do I want to do now?"* question.

Perhaps you didn't walk away from your dreams. Perhaps you're just in a place in your life where you've achieved everything you wanted and you're wondering, what's next? Or perhaps you stopped dreaming all together and you're just getting through the days.

Regardless where you may find yourself, you get to dream again – *if you want to*.

LET GO OF WHAT COULD HAVE BEEN

When track runner Derek Redmond was a teen, his dream was to be a record-breaking Olympic Gold Medalist. He trained hard and was well on his way. While running in the semifinals of the 1992 Olympic Games, a short distance from the finish line, his hamstring snapped causing him to fall to the ground in excruciating pain. When the stretcher-bearers came to take him off the field, he refused to go with them because he wanted to finish his race. As he was limping along the track, his father managed to get past security and helped him finish the race. They later learned that injury ended his career as a professional runner.

Dreams don't die; however, sometimes they do. It may sound contradictory, but it's not. There are times when the dream you've been working towards is no longer an option in the form you were pursuing; however, the dream to fully live out your God-given purpose never dies.

Derek's dream of becoming an Olympic Gold medal track runner died on the field that day, but the dream to be great stayed very much alive. Instead of giving up, he became a part of the Great Britain national basketball team and reached division 1 in the Great Britain rugby team. According to Wikipedia, he now serves as Director of Development for Sprints and Hurdles for UK Athletics and also works as a motivational speaker.

FORGIVE YOURSELF

Things happen, some you can control and other's you can't. *Are you angry with yourself for the choices you have made? Do you constantly beat yourself up?* If so, you have to let go to move forward.

Part of letting go is learning to forgive. Part of forgiving is forgiving ourselves, an overlooked but necessary piece of the puzzle.

For a long time, what held me back was my anger and disappointment in myself. I made choices and investments that led to debt, frustration and wasted time. I allowed fear and other people's opinions to hold me back. And I allowed insecurity to cause me to procrastinate and self-sabotage. Since I allowed those things, there wasn't anyone to be upset with but myself.

I had to get to a place where I realized that I did the best I could with where I was, what I had and what I knew at the time. I also had to realize that I could make new choices now, which could lead to new realities.

Let go of the couldas, wouldas and shouldas and acknowledge yourself for all you have been able to accomplish thus far. Chances are, you're further than you think you are and further than you give your yourself credit for.

You get to dream again, so do it. Dream. Don't allow the choices of your past or for opinions to define you. Either go after an old dream or dream a new dream. You never know what will happen or what adventure a new dream will take you on.

NOW WHAT

1 FILL IN THE BLANK.

INSPIRATION IS _____

2 FOOD FOR THOUGHT.

If you have walked away from a dream,

- Have you forgiven yourself for not being where you thought you would be or should be?

- Are you ready to let go in order to move forward?

- Do you want to go after your old dream, a new dream, or a variation of the old?

- What are the next steps you are going to take to make that happen?

3 WRITE A BREAKUP LETTER TO FEAR. share yours.

Write a breakup letter to fear and submit it at **idaretodreamproject.com/dearfear.**

HOW TO DREAM

A New Dream

1 **MOURN WHAT COULD HAVE BEEN.** Give
yourself permission to experience your
emotions.

2 **BURY THE OLD DREAM.** Let go of what
could've been and put to rest *how you*
thought the dream was going to happen.

3 **FORGIVE.** Forgive yourself and everyone who
may have contributed to the death of your
dream.

4 **KNOW THAT IT'S NOT OVER.** The initial dream
may no longer be an option, but a variation
may still possible. *Explore alternatives.*

5 **DREAM A NEW DREAM.** Don't allow what you
think you should do or want keep you tied to
an old dream.

6 **SAY YES MORE.** Say yes to new experiences
and things you wouldn't normally consider.
Surround yourself with dreamers and people
who are excited about life and passionate
about what they're doing.

7   **EMBRACE THE TEMPORARY.** Do something for now. You don't have to make a life decision. If there is something that excites you now, then explore it now.

8   **DON'T GET STUCK IN THE TEMPORARY.** Give yourself a time frame to explore different possibilities. When your time is up, decide if you want to continue down this path or explore a new one.

9   **SUPPORT ANOTHER DREAMER.** While you're deciding what your next step may be, support someone else in making their dreams a reality.

10 **HAVE FUN.** Relax and find joy in the journey.

DARE TO PURSUE

idaretodreamproject.com · 🅾 f 🅣 @idaretodreamproject

DARE TO SAY YES TO
PURSUING YOUR DREAMS
BECAUSE YOU CAN.
BECAUSE YOU MUST.
BECAUSE WHY NOT.

D

THE GREATEST THINGS IN LIFE
DON'T HAPPEN BY DEFAULT,
THEY ARE ACTIVE CHOICES. SO,
DECIDE.

DECIDE

REALITY CHECKUP		
For the sake of your dreams, are you willing to:		
	YES	**NO**
Invest your time, energy and resources?	☐	☐
Do things you that may terrify you?	☐	☐
Say yes to things you don't feel prepared for?	☐	☐
Risk failure?	☐	☐
Give up the safety of the familiar?	☐	☐
Admit you need help and ask for it?	☐	☐
Separate from friends?	☐	☐
Be judged and misunderstood?	☐	☐
Keep moving forward even if everyone around you thinks you should stop?	☐	☐

If you mostly answered yes, you're most likely prepared to pay the cost of yes.

Like with most potentially life-changing decisions, deciding whether or not to pursue your dreams can feel like a game of tug-of-war with faith, *the underdog*, versus fear, *the bully*. Fear will present so many valid objections and challenges that between the doubts in your mind and the opinions of others, you don't have to search hard to find reasons not to pursue. However, *in the midst of all the reasons you could say no, will you dare to pursue?*

IT TAKES COURAGE

Understand that beyond the financials, there is a cost to saying yes.

Pursuing your dreams will require you to invest your time, energy and resources. It may take a toll socially and emotionally, disrupt your norm and put you in a place where you are constantly uncomfortable and being stretched.

When I got my master's degree, my mom had certain expectations for me, and a well-paying nine-to-five job was one of them. My decision to pursue entrepreneurship full-time was not part of her plans. It wasn't part of mines either, but pursuing your dreams will change things.

There are people you will have to distance yourself from and those who will distance themselves from you. If you're married or in a relationship, your yes can change the dynamics of that relationship also, for better or for worse – that will be up to you and your partner to decide, but change is inevitable because you will change as a result of the journey.

In the midst of the cost and all the changes that will take place, it's your **why***, *the motivation and driving force that compels you to pursue,* that helps you stay focus and that reminds you that the cost is worth it. Without a clear *why* you may start to resent the process and sacrifices, be envious of others, and even rebel against all the demands one day.

THE TEMPTATION TO QUIT

Sometimes I ask myself, *if I knew in advance what it would take to make my dreams a reality, would I have still said yes?*

I would love to say that my answer would be, "*Absolutely*!"; however, sometimes it wasn't. There were *many* times when I was tempted to quit because of the cost and the disappointments along the way. But since this was a dream I believed in, I had to find ways to keep moving forward while every doubt, fear and insecurity was uprooted and constantly thrown in my face by me, by others, and by my results.

You will have moments when you'll just want to cry or scream. When those moments come, you need to be okay with not being okay, whether it's for a few minutes or a couple of days. Allow yourself a safe space and outlet to go through your emotions without any judgment. Otherwise, the emotional build up may manifest as attitude, anger, bitterness and rudeness. It may leave you saying or needing to say "I'm sorry."

As challenging as it can be sometimes, the process is not meant to take you out. It will test your commitment, but it will also strengthen you. During and after those tearful moments you will be forced to ask and answer the hard questions, like

- *Do you still want this?*
- *Do you still believe the dream is worth it?*
- *Are you willing to risk failure time and time again in order to realize it?*

As long as your answers to those questions are yes, keep moving forward. If not, then go find your yes.

The decision to pursue your dream is not a one-time yes. It's a series of continuous yeses you say daily and sometimes several times a day.

Every dream does not require the same sacrifice, but whatever yours require, will you say yes? Will you dare to pursue your dreams?

NOW WHAT

① FILL IN THE BLANK.

I MUST PURSUE MY DREAMS BECAUSE _____

_____

② FOOD FOR THOUGHT.

- What will the pursuit of your dream require?

- What changes will you be required to make?

- How do you think it will impact your relationships?

- What keeps you moving forward and saying yes to your dreams in the moments when you're tempted to quit?

③ WHAT DO YOU DARE TO DREAM? #shareyours.

Record and upload a video sharing what you dare to dream at **idaretodreamproject.com**.

HOW TO OVERCOME
Decision Paralysis

1 **BE AWARE.** Make sure you mark all the necessary dates and deadlines.

2 **BE INFORMED**. Gather as much information as you can.

3 **BE MINDFUL**. Know how this decision moves you towards your goal.

4 **BE BOLD**. Trust your instinct.

5 **BE INTENTIONAL.** Pick one or pick none – just make a conscious and intentional decision.

6 **DO NOT DELAY.** Understand that there is a window of opportunity, so decide in a timely manner.

7 **DO NOT BE HARD ON YOURSELF**. Understand that you won't always get it right, but it doesn't mean that you won't reach your goal.

8 **DO NOT PANIC**. Understand that you can course-correct.

9   **DO NOT OBSESS.** Understand that you won't always have all the information in advance, yet you still must decide.

10   **DO NOT LOSE FAITH.** Understand that whether you get it right or wrong, it's all a part of the journey.

FOR EVERYTHING YOU DO AND EVERY OPPORTUNITY YOU'RE PRESENTED WITH, TAKE TIME TO ASK YOURSELF, HOW DOES THIS LINE UP WITH MY VISION?

WHAT, WHY, WHO, & WHERE
FIGURE OUT HOW

When talking about dreams, the number one question every dreamer asks themselves and is asked by others is HOW?

How are you going to do it? How are you going to pay for it? How are you doing to get help? How? How? How? How? How?

It's a fair question, but it can also be a stressful one, especially when you're not sure of the answer. In fact, many people walk away from their dreams because they can't answer how.

As overwhelming as it seems at first, it's easier to answer HOW if you take the time to answer the four W questions, WHAT, WHY, WHO, and WHERE. All five questions are related. Understanding the relationships will help you when defining and deciding on HOW.

Clarity about WHAT, *your dream*, is strengthened by WHY, *your reason and motivation*. WHY, in turn, helps you focus your WHAT, which tells you WHO you have to be/become. Based on all that, WHERE, *your starting point,* helps you define your options. And everything together influences your HOW, your *actions and your approach*, which creates your RESULTS.

It really is simple. Just in case, let's break it down.

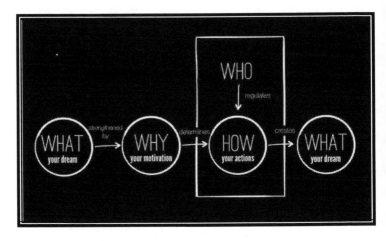

WHAT   *your dream, vision & your results*

WHY   *your reason and your motivation*

WHO   *who you are*
who you want to be
Who your dream requires you to be

WHERE   *your starting point*

HOW   *your actions and your approach*

SYSTEM OF CHECKS AND BALANCES

- WHAT, *your dream,* is strengthened by *your reason and motivation,* your WHY

- WHY helps focus your WHAT

- WHAT tells you WHO you have to be/become

- WHERE helps you define your options

- WHAT, WHY, WHO and WHERE influences HOW, *your actions and your approach,* which creates your RESULTS.

WHAT

You have to know WHAT you want. It may start out as a simple idea, but once you decide you are going to pursue, take time write out your vision with great detail. Once you've done that, create a vision board for your dream.

This is so fundamental, especially if you want to enroll the support of others. Since people can't see what's in your head, you must put your vision on paper.

Because dreamers are, well, dreamers, it's easy to get a little distracted during the vision writing stage. Part of what helps you focus and shape your dream is your WHY.

THE POWER OF WHY

WHY can be broken down into two categories, **excuses**, *why you will not and do not*, and **motives**, *why you must and you do*. Both are WHYs, but each inspire very different actions, which leads to very different results.

An excuse is a WHY that defends or justify lack of action or the decisions you made. On the other hand, a motivation is a WHY that explains your reason for doing something. It's what pushes you to take the necessary actions.

A motivating why, eliminates excuses. The clearer you are about why you're pursuing your dream, why it matters to you and the impact if can have in your life and the lives of others, the more motivated you'll be and the more action you'll take, which will help you create the results you want.

If your WHY is strong enough, then there's no obstacle big enough to stop you from going after and getting what you want. Your why is often strongest when it's connected to something bigger than you.

There's nothing wrong with starting out with a dream motivated by personal ambitions; however, don't be surprised if over time you notice a purpose-driven shift, where your focus is now on *how you can impact, contribute, or make a difference in the lives of others.*

WHO YOU ARE AND WANT TO BE

WHO you are, *your passions, purpose and personal experiences,* and WHO you want to be helps prevent you from compromising as you pursue your dreams. It serves as your boundary for how far you're willing to go to get what you want and it influences the choices you make and the opportunities you say yes to.

WHO you are is also important because no matter how good the idea is or how talented you are, bad character will cost you opportunities.

The same way you must take the time to define and write out your dream, you must take the time to also define and write out:

- WHO you are,
- WHO you want to be,
- WHO your dream requires you to be,

- and what character traits you need to have and work on.

It also includes defining how you show up and how you want to dress. Your wardrobe should reflect your personality, as well as your goals. It has nothing to do with how much money you spend or the labels you're wearing. It's about putting things together in a way that expresses who you are while positioning you for success.

HOW YOU CAN AND HOW YOU DO

HOW you go about pursuing your dreams is like using a GPS. In order to get from where you are to where you want to be, you must know WHAT the goal/destination is, as well as WHERE you are.

WHERE represents your starting point, which can include your experience and the resources and connections you have. As you get clearer about WHERE you are, you'll have a better idea of HOW you can, *the different options and possibilities that are available to help you get to where you want to be.*

How you go about pursuing your dream and the route you end up taking will be determined by your answers to the other questions:

- WHAT you want,

- WHAT kind of experiences you want to have getting there,

- WHY you want it,

- and WHO you are and want to be, *which will determine what you will or will not do to get there.*

Along the way you'll have to make a lot of decisions and have a lot of questions to answer. Some answers you'll know immediately. For the ones you don't, just start with what you do know and allow that to guide you in figuring out what you don't.

NOW WHAT

1 **FILL IN THE BLANK.**

I WANT (what) _____

BECAUSE (why) _____.

BECAUSE I AM (who) _____

I WON'T (boundaries) _____.

2 **FOOD FOR THOUGHT.**

- What is the motivation behind your dream?

- How will it impact your life and the lives of others?

- Who does your dream require you to become?

- What character traits do you need to work on in order to help you get to where you want to be?

3 **WHAT DO YOU DARE TO DREAM?** #shareyours.

Record and upload a video sharing what you dare to dream at **idaretodreamproject.com**.

HOW TO MAKE
Aligned Decisions

1   **CHECK FOR PROGRESS**. Does this move you towards or away from your vision?

2   **CHECK THE FINE PRINT**. Do you have all the information you need to make the best decision?

3   **CHECK FOR CONFLICT**. Does this conflict with your vision and/or deadline? Does it conflict with who you are and what you believe? Is this in line with how you want to do things and the kinds of experiences you want to have or create?

4   **CHECK YOUR MOTIVES.** What are your intentions? What are you hoping will come from this choice?

5   **CHECK FOR FOLLOW THROUGH.** Do you really intend on following through?

6   **CHECK FOR FEAR.** Why are you really saying yes/no? Is it a fear motivated decision?

7 **CHECK FOR NECESSITY**. Is this necessary to successfully achieve your goal?

8 **CHECK FOR COST**. How much will this cost (*financially, time, wise, etc.*)? Is it worth the investment?

9 **CHECK FOR ASSOCIATION**. Is this something you really want to be associated with?

10 **CHECK FOR POSITION**. Based on where I am, is this the best next step for me.

DOING THE RIGHT THING AT THE WRONG TIME CAN BE JUST AS DETRIMENTAL AS DOING THE WRONG THING AT ANY TIME.

DON'T OVERWHELM YOURSELF

Our natural need to go to the bathroom teaches us a lot about priorities. Lesson number one is "When you gotta go, you gotta go." You can try to hold it in, but if you keep delaying, eventually you won't be able to concentrate. And in spite of your best efforts, things might come out on their own. To avoid that, you learn very quickly how to put everything on hold and excuse yourself to relieve yourself.

That same principle and sense of urgency can be applied to your dreams. In order to focus and give the important things the attention they require, you have to learn to address the **pressing things***, *things demanding immediate attention.*

With so much continuously demanding our attention, how can you tell which is pressing?

By learning to listen.

- *What is consuming your mind right now?*

- *What do you keep coming back to?*

- *What do you keep thinking about when you're working on something else?*

Those are clues about pressing things you need to address.

When I started working on this book, it was not the most ideal time at all. Yet, in the midst of everything going on, I knew this was a pressing priority. I had to completely unplug for months to get it done. It wasn't until I got closer to completion, did I start to see why it was so pressing to write this book. **Focusing on the pressing simplifies the important**.

Turns out the writing and editing process were crucial in helping me get the clarity I needed for everything, from my branding to the long-term vision for what I wanted to create.

STATE OF FLOW

Finding the balance between the pressing and the important and trying to do everything when it needs to be done can feel overwhelming at times. As you look at your life, you will start to realize you are either in a state of flow, a state of the runs or a state of constipation.

The **state of flow*** is *rhythmic progress accompanied by a sense of peace and an inner knowing that all is as it should be*. You're setting goals, meeting deadlines, producing tangible results, stretching yourself, but not taking on too much. There's no straining and minimal pushing is required. Even if there are moments when a push is necessary, it usually comes in the end and allows for the completion of the process.

When you're in flow, you're aware of the time; you're in the right position; you're open and relaxed and willing to let go, which includes knowing when to let go of people and ideas and when to spend. It also includes knowing when to release certain products and aspects of your projects. Timing is critical because **doing the right thing at the wrong time can be just as detrimental as doing the wrong thing at any time.**

STATE OF THE RUNS

Too much flow and you may find yourself in a **state of the runs***, *the release or attempt to do too much at once that results in stress and overwhelm for yourself and others.* This tends to happen the closer you are to launching. You're so excited about what you have been working on, you want to release it all. Without the right system in place, releasing too much at once can cause you unnecessary stress and can compromise what you are working on.

Other causes include:

1   **AN OVERWHELMING FLOW OF IDEAS.** We get all types of ideas – from average to good to great. The danger lies in the inability to distinguish between the three and the attempt to execute them all, and often, all at once.

2   **INSECURITY AND LACK OF FEEDBACK.** When you're not getting the feedback you want, it can lead to insecurities and may

cause you to launch projects and ideas prematurely in hope of getting a response or reaction from people.

3   **COMPARING YOURSELF TO OTHERS**. Instead of focusing on your own goals and strategies, you try to do what you see others doing.

If you're in a state of the runs, take inventory. Identify what you need to focus on that will move you towards your goal. Remember, it's not about quantity, but about investing time in developing great ideas into exceptional realities.

STATE OF CONSTIPATION

Anyone who has ever experienced physical constipation knows it's painful. You're backed up, uncomfortable, agitated. You know you have to go; you want to go; at the same time, you're afraid to go, because it's probably going to hurt.

The **state of constipation*** is no different. It is *overwhelm brought on by a lack of progress, completion and results*. You are backed up on deadlines, projects, and promises. You're on edge and unfocused. If left unaddressed, it can not only cripple your progress, but make you a toxic, negative person.

Some of the more common causes of this type of overwhelm includes fear, incompletes, too many opinions, over-commitment, and lack of decision-making. Other causes include:

1   **I.G.S. – INFORMATION GATHERING SYNDROME**, obsessive information gathering that delays progress. It usually stems from insecurity and feelings of inadequacy and can lead to decision paralysis due to an overwhelming amount of options.

2   **SHADE OF BLUE SYNDROME**, an obsession over minute and sometimes-insignificant details, which can be fixed down the line.

3   **COMPARISITIS**, comparing yourself to others, which can lead to insecurity, low self-esteem, lack of motivation and competition. You may find that you're either putting someone else down to feel better about yourself or you're putting yourself down.

4   **DISEASE TO PLEASE**, a desperate desire to fit in and be accepted to the point where you make decisions based on whether or not others would approve, even if it compromises the goals you're working toward. It's also known as **the shoulda***, *the overwhelming need to do what you or someone else feels you should be doing, instead of what you want to be doing.*

5   **IMITATIONITIS**, trying to be something or someone you're not. It's usually a result of admiring someone or something to the

point you try to copy, even when it's not authentic to who you really are.

6   **CRISSCROSS MINDSET**, when you're driven by material wealth instead of purpose. You start confusing **success***, *the fulfilling of your goal or purpose*, with the outcomes of success, which includes but are not limited to money, influence, impact, legacy, certain freedoms and luxuries, a certain lifestyle, etc.

7   **SELF-CRITISM AND JUDGMENT,** speaking to yourself in a demoralizing way that robs you of confidence and makes you blind to your accomplishments.

As you look over the list, notice that most of the causes have to do with either your mindset or your actions (*or lack thereof*). If you learn to monitor and manage your thoughts and to take the right actions at the right time, you will be able to establish and maintain a state of flow. Just beware of **mylanta moments***, *quick fixes which lead to temporary relief without necessarily solving the problem*.

This journey is not a race where you have to finish first or fast, but it's about you doing what you have to do, when you have to do it, as best as you can do it, so that you can finish. **Be patient with yourself**.

NOW WHAT

1 **FILL IN THE BLANK.**
WHEN I AM OVERWHELMED I _____

_____

2 **FOOD FOR THOUGHT.**
- What state are you in?

  ❑ A State of Flow, where you're setting goals and meeting deadlines in stress-free way.

  ❑ A State of Constipation, where you're over-whelmed because you're behind on tasks and deadlines.

  ❑ A State of the Runs, where you're over-whelmed because you're simply trying to do too much.

- If you're not in a state of flow, what are three steps you can take to get to a state of flow?

3 **WHAT DO YOU DARE TO DREAM?** #shareyours.
Record and upload a video sharing what you dare to dream at **idaretodreamproject.com**.

HOW TO GET BACK TO A
State of Flow

1 **TAKE INVENTORY.** What are the pressing things that are demanding your attention right now and that if you complete will have the biggest impact in moving you forward?

2 **SORT AND COMPLETE.** Go through what you need to do and sort out what needs to be completed, deleted, outsourced, or filed away for the future.

3 **K.I.S.S. YOUR DREAMS.** Keep It Super Simple. How can you simplify what you're currently working on?

4 **BREAK OLD PROMISES.** If there are things you said yes to but now realize you cannot honor, reach out to the respective people and let them know. Take responsibility. Be honest. Apologize. Do better moving forward.

5 **SAY NO.** You're going to have to say no to opportunities that seem great and to people who won't always understand. Who and what are some things you need to say no to?

6   **ASK, ASK, ASK.** Ask for the support and resources you need.

7   **CREATE SYSTEMS AND CHECKLISTS.** It's easier for people to help you, if you know what you need and can give clear instructions.

8   **GET LOVE. GIVE LOVE.** When you feel loved, do something fun, or just enjoy a nice meal in good company, oxytocin, *the hormone of love*, is released, which balances cortisone, *the stress hormone*. You will also get the same benefits when you give love to others. So, get love and give love.

9   **CREATE A CHEER SQUAD.** Who are the people you can regularly connect with who will cheer you on by celebrating your work and encouraging you during your missteps? Who are the ones *you* can be a cheerleader for?

10 **STEP AWAY.** Take time out for you. Take a break, unplug, go on a vacation, and then come back with a fresh perspective.

PEOPLE NEED PEOPLE.
PERIOD.

YOU ARE NOT IN THIS ALONE
GET CONNECTED

Can you hold my hand as I push?
As exciting as this is, I'm in a lot of pain.
There are a lot of tears and complications
    may arise.
I'm frustrated and making a mess of things.
I'm overwhelmed; emotional and suddenly
    overcome with fear and doubt in my
    ability to do this.
In between the pressures and the demands,
    I'm worrying about the future.
I guarantee you, I will say things that don't
    really sound like me.
I may get an attitude.
I may talk crazy and seem unreasonable and
    overly sensitive.
I don't mean to make excuses, but I'm
    scared.
In the midst of all that I just want to know, can
    you hold my hand as I push?
Are you willing to stand by my side even if it
    causes you pain?
Are you prepared to talk me through my
    doubts and my fears?
Will you tell me how great I'm doing and
    encourage me to keep going?

Can you stand by my side and be silent with
*   me?*
Do you promise not to judge me and throw
*   my shortcomings in my face?*
Will you help me remember that I can do this and
*   that it's possible?*
Can you hold my hand as I push?
Can You Hold My Hands, Valerie Jeannis, 2014

Having a dream and deciding to pursue that dream is exciting. The possibilities, the people, the celebrations, the lessons learned – it's all amazing. At the same time, it can be the most challenging thing you ever do.

On July 4, 1952, Florence Chadwick was on her way to becoming the first woman to swim the Catalina Channel. She fought and swam her way through dense fog, freezing cold, and sharks on her way to the shore. One of her biggest challenges was that every time she looked through her goggles, all she could see was the dense fog. After swimming through all those obstacles, she reached a point where she decided to quit.

After she was pulled out of the water, she learned that she was only a half a mile from the shoreline. Half a mile!

She later said in an interview, "I'm not making excuses, (but) if I had seen the land, I could have made it." She gave up, not because she was unable to go the distance, but because she couldn't see the end pass the fog.

Two months later, she went back and swam the Catalina Channel again. This time, in spite of the bad weather, she was so focused that not only did she accomplish her goal, she beat the men's record by two hours!

You'll never want to quit more than when you are closest to the finish line. That's when everything will seem too hard and when you'll suddenly feel as though you can't go another step or take another hurdle or setback. You can get so worn out by the process that you have **blurred faith***, the *momentary loss of faith which makes it hard to see that it's possible to get from where you are to where you want and are called to be.* It can be caused by doubt, fear, a lack of perceived progress and success, or just pure exhaustion. Your faith in the possibility will return, especially as you make progress, see results and get encouragement. However, **your challenge is to believe and maintain your faith, often in spite of what you see.** In those moments it's important that you have people you can turn to, who will help you keep hope alive. It's important that you're connected.

ESSENTIAL CONNECTIONS

Pursuing your dream requires you to say yes before anyone else does and even if no one else does. At the same time, it's not a journey you can do on your own. Even if you're an independent person, it doesn't change the fact you need to be connected.

Connections are how we learn, grow, give

and receive. Four essential connections you need to maintain as you pursue are connections with God, yourself, your dream, and others.

CONNECTION WITH GOD

The connection with God is often overlooked because it's spiritual and can be confused with religion, when truly, it's about relationship. **It's based less on what we can see and more on what we believe.**

It's about faith, a *well-grounded confidence that what you hope for will actually happen.*

Had it not been for my faith, I never would've made it this far. It was my relationship and friendship with God that sustained and continues to inspire and propel me forward, especially in the moments when I was tempted to quit.

Without a doubt faith is necessary, but *faith in what?* It's a question we must all answer for ourselves.

What is the source of your faith? What is it that lets you know that what you want and what you're going after is possible for you? What is it that lets you know you can do this?

The stronger your faith, the more stable and resilient you will be.

CONNECTION WITH YOURSELF

In order to truly connect with yourself, you have to be true to yourself. You can't hold back or apologize for who you are. You also have to take care of yourself.

As much as you love your dream, if you want to maintain your enthusiasm and passion, then you must step away regularly. It can't always be about the dream and you can't constantly be giving and not make time to recharge all aspects of yourself – your mind, body and spirit.

Because it's easier to take time out when you know what your options are, create a list of things you like to do to unwind and actually schedule time in your calendar to have fun and recharge. You get to make yourself a priority.

CONNECTION WITH YOUR DREAM

A life coach once asked me, *"What does a speaker do?"* Without skipping a beat, I said, "They market themselves, connect with others, invest in trainings, and prepare talks."

The coach just looked at me and said, "Speakers speak." Turns out, I was so focused on courses, branding, and networking, I rarely did the thing I wanted to do – speak!

It's possible to neglect the dream while you are actually working *on* the dream. You have to find ways to actively do the things you dream of doing, even if you can't do it to the scale you want to yet. If you want to be a speaker, speak. If you want to be a singer, sing. If you want to be an author, write. If you want to be an artist, create. You see where I'm going.

CONNECTION WITH OTHERS

People need people. Period.

There's a reason why so many are willing to pay hundreds and thousands of dollars to attend seminars and join masterminds and coaching groups. It's because there's something incredibly powerful and synergetic about being a part of a supportive community of like-minded people connected through a shared experience who understand you.

A support group is:

- A place where you can go for support, feedback and guidance,

- A place to simply be without pretense or feeling the need to "fake it",

- A place where you can share your victories and be celebrated, your frustrations and be listened to, your disappointments and be comforted, your challenges and be guided,

- A place of connection where you just fit.

Having a support group is so important that if you can't find one you really connect with, you should consider starting your own. Part of my vision is to create both an online and offline community for the ones who dare – the ones with big dreams, entrepreneurial spirit, and a taste for adventure. A community where we encourage, challenge and celebrate each other. That's the heart behind the *I Dare to Dream Project*.

As you maintain your essential connections with God, yourself, your dreams, and others, the speed and magnitude of your success and impact will increase exponentially. Neglect any one of those connections and you'll lose the benefits that come from that connection. So, stay connected.

NOW WHAT

1 FILL IN THE BLANK.

I FEEL MOST CONNECTED TO MYSELF WHEN _____

_____

2 FOOD FOR THOUGHT.

- Of the four essential connections, which is your strongest? Weakest?

3 STRENGTHEN YOUR CONNECTIONS.

Take action to strengthen and maintain your strong connections and work on your weak ones.

❑ Connection to God.
Reflect on who/what you believe in beyond yourself.

❑ Connection with Yourself.
Create a vision board of who you want to be

❑ Connection with Your Dreams.
Schedule time daily/weekly to do the thing that you dream of doing.

❑ Connection with Others.
If you don't already have a network of support, start exploring what your options are.

4 WHAT DO YOU DARE TO DREAM? #shareyours.

Record and upload a video sharing what you dare to dream at **idaretodreamproject.com**.

HOW TO
Maintain Connections

WITH GOD

1 **DECIDE WHAT YOU BELIEVE IN.** What is your position when it comes to faith? God? Spirituality?

2 **COMMUNICATE.** How do you connect with God? How does God speak to you? How can you create more opportunities to connect and communicate?

3 **FIND A FAITH COMMUNITY.** It's important to be with like-minded people who encourage and strengthen your faith.

WITH YOURSELF

4 **CELEBRATE AND ACKNOWLEDGE YOURSELF.** How do you celebrate when you have an achievement?

5 **MAKE YOURSELF A PRIORITY.** It's ok to regularly put yourself first. Don't hesitate to say no when you have to and yes when you want to.

WITH YOUR DREAM

6   **START WHERE YOU ARE**. Don't wait until you have everything you want. Use what you have to get started until you get what you need.

7   **FOCUS ON YOUR WHY**. Constantly remind yourself why you said yes and why you continue to say yes.

8   **KNOW YOUR IMPACT**. Celebrate and acknowledge progress and the impact your pursuit has had in your life and the life others.

WITH OTHERS

9   **FOCUS ON CREATING WIN WINS**. Aim for all your relationships to be win wins. Don't just be a taker and don't just be a giver.

10   **BE HONEST**. Communicate your desires and address issues as they come up.

GREATNESS IS A CHOICE
AND IT'S AVAILABLE TO YOU.
IF YOU WANT IT, CHOOSE IT.

GO FOR GREAT

Growing up school came easy for me. Without putting in much effort, I was always an honor student – not the best, but among the best. It wasn't until my eighth-grade graduation, as I watched the same students get called time and time again for actually being the best in their subjects, did I start to realize what complacency and laziness caused me to miss out on. I was good, but I wasn't great. Not because I couldn't be, but because I didn't choose to be.

It's one thing to decide to do something. It's another thing entirely to make a decision to go for great. **Greatness does not just happen.** It's an active choice that goes beyond resting on your talent and abilities. It requires you to be correctable, unquenchable, and to own your extraordinary.

BE CORRECTABLE

Your ability to be great and to excel in all aspects of your life is directly proportional to your ability to receive and implement feedback. You must be correctable and others must be able to tell you the truth without fear of repercussions. It's not always easy because our emotions get involved and we can view feedback as an attack instead of a growth opportunity.

To make receiving feedback easier, check yourself.

1   **CHECK YOUR MINDSET.** Are you open to receiving feedback?

2   **CHECK YOUR PRIDE.** Resist the urge to defend yourself.

3   **CHECK YOUR RESPONSE.** How do you feel about the feedback? Are you frustrated, hurt, convicted? Why do you feel that way?

4   **CHECK YOUR ASSUMPTIONS**. Realize that it's not personal. The person giving the feedback may be as uncomfortable giving it as you are receiving it.

5   **CHECK THE MOTIVE.** Is the purpose of the feedback to support you and help you grow?

6   **CHECK YOUR UNDERSTANDING.** Ask clarifying follow up questions or repeat what you heard to make sure you heard and interpreted correctly.

7   **CHECK YOUR ATTITUDE**. There's always something positive that can be taken away, whether it's a lesson, a nugget, or a stronger conviction.

8　**CHECK YOUR TIMING.** You don't always have to answer immediately. If you need to, take time to process the information and then respond.

9　**CHECK YOUR WOUNDS.** Sometimes feedback hurts, whether it was intentional or not. So, make sure that you are ok.

10　**CHECK FOR GROWTH.** How can this feedback serve you? What will you take and what will you leave?

Feedback does not always equal truth; however, if you learn to listen and check it for truth before you decide to take it or leave it, it can be the difference between success and failure.

BE UNQUENCHABLE

Part of the reason greatness is so celebrated is the recognition of the commitment, dedication, focus, and hunger it takes to get there. To be great, you have to be unquenchable.

You have to refuse to be satisfied with less than your best. Refuse to be deterred or silenced by doubts, insecurity, or failure. Refuse to allow people, fear or circumstances to pollute your mind, faith, and dreams.

When you choose to go for great, you're choosing to be a trailblazer and to go places many aren't willing to go because of the kind of investment required. You won't always be alone, but you must be willing to go though none go with you. Fortunately, you'll meet other trail-blazers along the way who'll become friends, advisors and sometimes, even a spouse.

OWN YOUR EXTRAORDINARY

Lastly, **own your extraordinary***. *Recognize your genius and contribution and don't apologize for your, gifts, talents, accomplishments, what you want or what you have.* Don't be dependent on the praises or validation of others. And always know your worth, demand your worth and charge your worth.

In short, when you're owning your extra-ordinary, you'll have an internal confidence that permeates through all you do.

YOU GOT THIS

Greatness is a choice and it's available to you.

So, to the ones who want more than the lives that they're living and who are willing to do something about it, to the ones who recognize that they are more than they have allowed themselves to become, to the ones with big dreams, entrepreneurial spirit and a taste for adventure - I wrote this book to you because I believe in you.

I ask of you the same thing I ask of myself, to go for it. In spite of how you feel, the magnitude of the task, or how long it takes for you to figure it out, just go for it.

So what if they think you're a delusional dreamer? *Just don't let it be true.*

So what if they think you're wasting your time? *Just care less.*

So what if you fail? *Just become an extraordinary failure.*

So what if you don't have everything you need? *Just decide and watch provision follow.*

So what if you get stuck sometimes? *Just take steps to get back in flow.*

So what if they don't believe in you? *Just believe in yourself and do it anyway.*

There will be challenges along the way. There will be a hundred reasons you can say no and a thousand times when you'll want to quit. My encouragement to you is to in spite of it all, *Do It Anyway.* Pursue anyway. Go after it anyway. And do it your way.

1 **BECAUSE YOU CAN.** You really and truly got this. In spite of any and everything, you can do it.

2 **BECAUSE YOU MUST.** Your dream matters. To your life and to the lives of others you don't even know yet and that you may never know.

3   **BECAUSE WHY NOT**. Seriously, why not? This can be the start of your greatest adventure or simply lessons learned. Either way, you'll never have to wonder, *"What if I tried?"* Instead, you get to talk about what happened after you said yes.

This is your one life to live. You can play small or you can dare to dream and then dare to pursue unapologetically.

I hope you choose the latter.

from one unquenchable dreamer to another,

Valerie

And when they doubt
(and they might)
And when they tell you you can't
(and some will)
And even then "they" is really YOU
(and it often is)

DO IT ANYWAY

Because you can
Because you must
Because why not

THE *Rebel's* MANIFESTO

© Valerie Jeannis 2017

NOW WHAT

1 FILL IN THE BLANK.
I WILL _____.

2 FOOD FOR THOUGHT.
- Decide to dare to dream.
- Decide to dare to pursue.
- Decide to do it all unapologetically.

3 CONNECT WITH US ONLINE.
Website – **idaretodreamproject.com**
Instagram - **@idaretodreamproject**
               @ValerieJeannis

4 LEAVE A REVIEW.
I would love to hear from you. *What did you love? What were your takeaways? How has the message helped you on your journey?*

Post your feedback on Amazon.com, send an email to **hello@ValerieJeannis.com** or my favorite, send me mail at 55 West 116th Street, PO Box 256, New York, NY 10026. If you write it, I'll read it ☺

5 WHAT DO YOU DARE TO DREAM? #shareyours.
If you haven't already, record and upload your video sharing what you dare to dream at **idaretodreamproject.com**.

I DARE TO DREAM PROJECT

idaretodreamproject.com   @idaretodreamproject

WHAT DO YOU DARE TO DREAM?

Submit a video sharing your dreams
and be a part of our documentary

WE ARE THE ONES WHO DARE

THE FUN. THE FEARLESS. THE PURPOSE-DRIVEN.
THE UNAPOLOGETIC.

We want more than the lives that we're living and we're doing something about it.

We accept the possibility that we may be talked about, misunderstood or rejected.

We take drastic measures to make our dreams happen and willingly walk the road less traveled.

We choose daily to care less about other people's opinions and to break up with fear.

We are relentless. Unquenchable dreamers. Extraordinary failures. Purpose-driven rebels.

We are a community.

We celebrate, support and encourage each other. We stand by each other and for each other.

We go for great. We own our extraordinary.

We dare to dream and dare to pursue our dreams unapologetically.

And we have fun along the way.

@ Valerie Jeannis 2015

ACKNOWLEDGEMENTS

TO MY MOM. Thank you for everything, everything, everything. I am beyond grateful. I love you and would not trade you for the world.

TO MY PASTOR, BISHOP CARLTON T. BROWN. Thank you for being a shepherd who was willing to take time away from the ninety-nine to listen and speak life to the one.

TO MY FRIENDS, CHEERLEADERS AND ACCOUNTABILITY PARTNERS. TO THOSE WHO WERE THERE FROM THE BEGINNING AND THOSE WHO WERE THERE FOR A SEASON. Thank you for your time, encouragement, friendship and unwavering faith in me. The journey would have looked a lot different without you each in my corner.

TO MY CHAMPIONS, CHEERLEADERS, MENTORS AND ADVISORS – I don't know how to begin to say thank you to each and every single one of you for the role you played. I remember it all and have written it all in my journals. For now, allow me instead to simply acknowledge you by name – Liz Abzug, Ermany Beaubrun, Shana Bennett, Joan Byrd, Ifetaya Deck, September Dorhman, Ed Dowling, Sandra Grace, Saundra Heath, Robert Howitt, Nehemie and Ernest Janvier, Jessica Laporte, Carla Brown Madison, Dr. Jeffrey Magee, Ann McIndoo, Pam Bouma Miller, Samantha Roseline Prindilus, Yverose Prindilus, Allyn Reid, Jennifer Rosenwald, Caroll Schwartz, Geralde Sully, Claudine Williams, Diane Williams.

TO MY UNQUENCHABLE SELF. It wasn't easy, but it was worth it. I am beyond proud of you and I 100% believe in you.

TO GOD, MY BUSINESS COACH & FOREVER FRIEND. Thank you for entrusting me with this dream and assignment and for holding my hands through it all.

TO YOU, THE READER. Thank you for having this conversation with me and allowing me to share some of the things I learned along the way. By all means, do write me, reach out on social, send an email or actual mail. I would love to hear from you. If you write it, I will read it ☺.

Post your feedback on Amazon.com, send an email to **hello@ValerieJeannis.com** or my favorite, send me mail at 55 West 116th Street, PO Box 256, New York, NY 10026. If you write it, I'll read it ☺

A WOMAN
ON A MISSION

idaretodreamproject.com 📘📷 @idaretodreamproject

AUTHOR AND MOTIVATIONAL SPEAKER
VALERIE JEANNIS IS ON A MISSION TO DARE
YOU TO PURSE YOUR DREAMS
UNAPOLOGETICALLY

Valerie Jeannis is the creative force behind *I Dare to Dream Project* – a movement, with a powerful documentary at its core - inspiring women and girls to dare to dream, share their dreams, and pursue their dreams unapologetically.

With a mandate to disrupt, challenge and inspire, Valerie is continuously finding fun and unconventional ways to empower individuals to take action on their dreams. One of those ways being the user-generated documentary, where women and girls of all ages and from all walks of life are asked to record and submit a video answering the question - WHAT DO YOU DARE TO DREAM?

Valerie has authored several books including, *Dare to Dream: The Dreamer's Manifesto, Diary of a Dreamer, Conversations with God, and I Am Beautiful.*

She is also an international speaker and rapidly becoming a highly sought-after voice in the youth and college market and faith communities. She specializes in leadership, personal development and confidence-building.

Valerie teaches and conducts experiential workshops based on her books, the Dare to Dream philosophy, and her unconventional approaches to realizing the dream.

Her interactive presentations and down-to-earth speaking style are just some of the reasons audiences love her and students *themselves* arrange to have her brought in.

LEARN MORE about how to book Valerie for your next event at **www.idaretodreamproject.com** or email **info@idaretodreamproject.com.**

COMING SOON

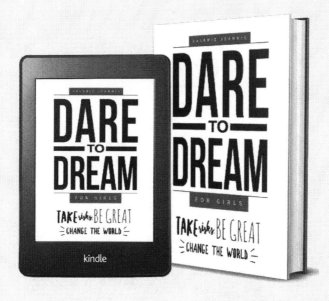

DARE TO DREAM
FOR GIRLS

TAKE chances. BE GREAT
CHANGE THE WORLD

Notes &

Thoughts

Use the next few pages to write down your notes and thoughts about whatever may have come up for you.

UNAPOLOGETIC PRESS

Made in the USA
Lexington, KY
22 November 2019